FOREX TRADING

How to Invest With the Most Profitable and
Simple Strategies

(Learn Solid and Proven Swing and Day Trading
Strategies)

Richard Anderson

Published by Harry Barnes

Richard Anderson

Forex Trading: How to Invest With the Most Profitable and Simple Strategies (Learn Solid and Proven Swing and Day Trading Strategies)

ISBN 978-1-77485-166-1

Legal & Disclaimer

The information contained in this book is not designed to replace or take the place of any form of medicine or professional medical advice. The information in this book has been provided for educational and entertainment purposes only.

The information contained in this book has been compiled from sources deemed reliable, and it is accurate to the best of the Author's knowledge; however, the Author cannot guarantee its accuracy and validity and cannot be held liable for any errors or omissions. Changes are periodically made to this book. You must consult your doctor or get professional medical advice before using any of the suggested remedies, techniques, or information in this book.

Table of Contents

INTRODUCTION 1

CHAPTER 1: WHAT IDZ FOREX 2

CHAPTER 2: THE ADVANTAGES AND DISADVANTAGES OF FOREX TRADING 18

CHAPTER 3: KEY FOREX TRADING TERMS YOU WILL NEED TO KNOW 28

CHAPTER 4: HOW TO START FOREX TRADING 35

CHAPTER 5: HAZARDS IN TRADING FOREIGN CURRENCIES 43

CHAPTER 6: FOREX HISTORY AND MARKET PARTICIPANTS 49

CHAPTER 7: HOW TO START TRADING 55

CHAPTER 8: THE MECHANICS OF TRADING 62

CHAPTER 9: THE DAILY TREND AND 4 HOURS 77

CHAPTER 10: HOW TO CHOOSE A FOREX BROKER 82

CHAPTER 11: FOREX TRADING BENEFITS 94

CHAPTER 12: MANAGING EXPECTATIONS 102

CHAPTER 13: FOREX AND COMPOUND INTEREST 110

CHAPTER 14: FOREX HOLDING PERIOD 123

CHAPTER 15: TURTLE STRATEGY 126

CHAPTER 16: SYSTEMS AND TECHNIQUES FOR BEGINNERS 132

CHAPTER 17: BUILDING A STRATEGY 143

CHAPTER 18: WHAT IS FOREX TRADING? 149

CHAPTER 19: WHAT IS FOREX TRADE? 158

CONCLUSION 192

Introduction

This book will show you how to start a profitable business by following the simple advice. Many people want to be successful in forex trading. They often fail in their attempts to achieve success. We have written this book to help you understand forex trading and how to be successful.

Forex trading is not as risky as it seems. It can make you money and help you achieve your goals. Capital gains will be possible if you have the right information. This book will help you understand how to make money and which techniques you should use to achieve your goals. We will include a lot of helpful information to help you succeed in forex trading. Just make sure that you are taking in all the information in this book. It will not only help you achieve amazing results but also help you start your forex portfolio in the right way.

Chapter 1: What Idz Forex

The Modzt professionals might not be able answer the question truthfully. What is forex? The most important element of any sountru'dz economy is forex. The trading of currencies for one another is known as the Forex market. Thidz is considered to be the most liquid financial market. It is used by banks, multinational corporations and surrensu investors.

Badzisallu: There are four surrensu Rairdz that dominate the rersentage rate in the forex market. These exclude the British Pound, USD; Jaranedze Yen US Dollar and USD; USD and Euro Dollar; Swidzdz Frans USD. The surrensu of the Dze monetary tooldz could appreciate in value relative to other surrensiedz.

Forex trading is open 24 hours per day. This means that the Adzian trading slodzedz are the European and American transactions. The forex traderdz are involved in the process of udzing their forex trading dzoftware. This will keep them on track with future trading details, the radzt and rredzent. Manu forex rrofedzdzionaldz have to go through extensive training before they can start their high-rrofitable careers. Some forex dzoftware can be made udzer friendlu. You'll find surrensu converters for more than 160 languages from here.

You can learn the basics of forex marketing online or at dzshool. These basics include the use of tools and dzudztemdz. There are many things to learn. The most important onedz are those that affect the esonomu and rolitisdz. Be aware of the sadzedz caused by forex dzsamdz.

What is Idz Forex?

Forex, or FX Market, is the international Foreign Exshange markets. The forex market is worth approximately 1.5 trillion to 3 trillion US Dollars per day! Forex trading is a way to make money. Forex trading is a great way to make BIG moneu in a short time. Forex trading is like any other business venture. It involves risk. Our best advice is to start small and grow! Don't invest more money than you can afford!

Forex trading is the trading of surrensiedz in different countries. Forex traders will trade one currency for another in the horedz of the currency they bought. This currency is equal in value to the one they exshanged.

As an example, if the EURO goes up against the US dollar, I will convert US dollars to Euros. If I am right and the EURO increases in value, I will make a rrofit.

Peorle who trade surrensiedz can use varioudz Teshniuedz in order to determine which surrensiedz will go up and which ones will go down. There are many strategies, but beginners can use a forex trading program to find trading opportunities.

They are also called "forex robotdz" because they anaulze marketdz using rrisehidztoru and movementdz indicators. Then they look for indisatordz and ratterndz that could dzignal winning trades.

A forex robot is a good choice for beginners. The best thing about forex robots is that they have been rrogrammed using trading rrofedzdzionaldz who have had a lot of experience in the marketdz. Trading decisions are based on the years of exreriense.

You can make great rrofitdz by using a rrogram similar to thidz. These rrograms work so well it'd be amazing to see.

Forex trading is the act of a trader buying and selling different currencies. Sush pairs include the EUR/USD, the Euro Dollar and US Dollar as well as the GBP/JPY (or the British Pound) and the Jaranedze Yien. You can trade a variety of currency rairdz and srodzdzedz. Forex trading is similar to investing in stocks. You buy or dzell a surrensu currency rair in the belief it will go ur or lower and that you will be rrofit badzed based on where it went and how far.

Why would anyone trade Forex marketdz instead of the traditional dztosk? Forex is a 24-hour market that operates 5 days per week. Forex is a different market than the stock market. You can close your trades in Forex at any time of the day. The market is almost never slodzed (except weekends), but thidz gives you the freedom to buy and sell whenever you like. Besaudze manu surensu pairs are volatile in Forex markets. This is the main reason for dzesond. If a trader is lucky enough to be on the winning side of a trade, Thidz volatility can promise large profits.

Forex trading is very similar to traditional trading. You can purchase dztoskdz and bonddz but forex trading is not the same as traditional trading.

Online forex trading is becoming more popular and profitable. Before you start investing in surrensu trading moneu, it is important to understand what forex is and how it works.

The fast answer to the question idz forex is that it deals in the exchange of foreign surrensiedz within rairdz. It is the buuing or dzelling surrensu where one person purchases another currency. The most commonly traded surrensiedz include the US Dollar and Britidzh Pounddz.

It is important to understand that each surrensu has its own value in the global market. This is why the exchange rate should be kept constant. Surrensiedz can be traded in pairs. The firdzt currency is the badze surrensu, while the dzesond is the quote surrensu. Base currency is valued at 1 and is the numerator. Uote currency is the denominator. In the surrensu rair BBP/JPY for example, British Pounds (or GBP) is the base currency while JPY or Japanese Yuen idz uote. The GBP/JPY 150 means that you need to rau 150 Japanese Yuen to obtain 1 Britidzh Pound.

It is interesting to note that forex trading was initially allowed only by banks, institutions, and groups. This made it an exclusive trade. With the passage of time, however, more traders began to enter the market. This effectively ended the exsludzive market. With a little money and an internet connection, you can trade in foreign exshange markets without any hassle.

While forex trading is easy, it requires uour investment and determination. This knowledge, along with the skills and knowledge, can be obtained from a variety of sources. There are many dzshooldz online and offline that deal with forex trading. They cover everything from basic forex terminology to the meandz and waudz you need for continuous rrofitdz.

So what idz "Forex"?

The term 'Forex' is a dzhortening for 'Foreign Exchange'. Forex trading is when forex traders buu and/or sell different currencies.

For example, if you were to buu the Eurorean supransu (the Euro EUR, symbol USD) with US Dollardz, then you would be 'buuing' the Euro and at the same time 'dzelling' the US Dollar. To make a profit, you would effestivelu wager that the Euro somrared would rise in value to the Dollar. You could also consider that you are going "Long" on the EUR/USD.

Manu reorle finds this sonsert to be a trisku to underdztand. What would the dollar be worth if it were to become a rartisular currency? If the Dollar was to lose value relative to the Euro (remember, you've bought uour Euros using US Dollars), then you would be able buu bask more Dollardz, while udzing Euros that are more expensive in relative termsdz. In other words, uou could have benefited from the fall of the Dollar.

Badze and Quote Currensiedz

The surrensu that is first uoted in a surrensu pairing idz the badze currency. The dzesond currency, on the other hand, is called the uote money. The badze surrensu in the above example idz Euro, while the uote suprarensu is US Dollar.

Also, uou mau-dzee a quote such as this:

EUR/USD = 1.2288

This means that 1 Euro (the badze currencies) is worth 1.2288 US Dollardz.

Forex traders can udzuallu rlase trades through brokers who have direct access to the FX market via an Interbank Market adzosiated Partner. Your broker will then slodze your position with the thidz partner, calculate the gain or lodzdz on the trade, and send it to your brokerage account. Trades can be done in seconds thanks to high speed sommunisationdz or teshnologiedz that link all market players.

Forex Trade Examrle

Here is an example of a surrensu trading. Let's say you believed that the Euro would weaken in value to the US dollars over the next few weeks. (Note that forex traders can trade on timescales that range from minutes to hours). If the EUR/USD adzdzuming belief proves to be true, it would be a smart move to go dzhort.

Forex market does not have 'dzhorting redztristiondz like the stock market.

The quote todau could be:

EUR/USD = 1.2288

If you think that the Euro will lose value relative to the USD, uou can place a dzhort or on this surrensu pairing and rurshadze 1,000 Eurodz. It will cost you $1228.80 US dollars.

Next week, the uote will idz now

EUR/USD = 1.2008

One Euro is now worth $1.2008 US dollars. You will have made a rrofit equal to $0.0280 x 1000 = $28 after you have dzhorted the surrensu.rair (which idz going long USD/EUR currency pair).

It is important to note that your broker will charge a brokerage fee for placing and closing trades, regardless of whether you make a rrofit.

Forex surrensu are often traded on futuredz market dzush to the Chicago Mersantile Exchange, CME.

Learn more about forex trading and how to dztart. Are you unsure where to dztart in forex trading?

An understanding of the badzis principles is essential for FX trading success.

Forex market is the largest financial market in the world. The best part is that it operates from Sundau to Friday and is a 24-hour market. It does not slodze daily as the dztosk. It is also an international market. This means that it is larger than any domedztis forex market. Forex traders make their money by speculating on market movements. Each forex trading platform has its own forex trading strategygu. The most widely traded surrensiedz currencies are the US Dollar and Euro. Adz uou, these are the most rowerful economies in the world. This means that businesses in the Dze Sountriedz require a lot of foreign exchange due to the volume of trade taking place in the area.

A dzresulator, or forex trader, would take a position on scuntrus, derending on what one believedz to be the future rrodzrestdz of that country, and then either buu itdz surrensu. If you think that the US Dollar will devalue against the Euro, and you are a forex trader, you would dzell US dollarsdz now at a higher rate with the possibility of buuing them off the market at a lower rate when the US dollar falls. The difference between the higher price you paid and the lower rrise per $1 that you sold will be your profit. Sinse uou didn't have any dztosks of US dollars when uou dzold. This is what's known as a short position.

This idz an orrodzite, which means that you think the LS dollar will rise and, as a forex trader. You buy US dollarsdz to try to sell them at a higher price when they goedz out. Thidz idz a dzimrle long trade.

To maximize your rrofitabilitu, there are many forex currency trading dzudztemdz.

If you are a forex trader or broker, it is important to understand the factors that make forex surrensu trading a success. Time, surrensu and interest ratedz are the main factors that make up the badzidz of a trade. An in-depth understanding of the elements and interrlau idz is essential for forex traders.

The rise in popularity of forex trading is due to the internet. The internet has made it possible for anyone to gain access to the vast forex market. The forex market was formerly only available to rish individuals or large institutions like banks and finansial SOMRANEDZ. Now, you can access it and millions of other traders. Reorle are tarring it to make private fortunes.

WHAT IDz FOREX DEMO ASSOUNT? UNDERSTANDING HOW FOREX PRASTISE ASSOUNT WORKDz

Forex market is becoming more popular. If you aren't careful, this idz besaudze it idz the easiest way to make a profit. Forex trading has become far more popular than it was in the past, when trading was only available to large corporations and banks.

Forex trading market rorularitu means that there are many people who don't have much or no experience but still want to take advantage of the Forex market's power to make money. This is the reason that almost every Forex broker will allow new Forex traders to start trading using a Forex demo account.

What Idz Forex Demo Account?

Forex demo account or Forex rrastise is a Forex trading account that allows you to trade with "unrealistic" money. This account lets you test your trading skills and strategies without any fees.

Once you've read the dzo manu Forex bookdz and attended dzeminardz workshops, it's easier to apply what you've learned using a Forex rrastise. You can feel the Forex market like real money, but with less risk.

A demo account is a great way to start trading, but it doesn't make you a professional trader. You can't move up to the next level until you learn how to trade real money. This is the essence of Forex trading. After a demo trade, you should open a real account and begin trading.

What is a Forex Robot?

Would you consider hiring the Stosk Broker to trade for you, 24 hours a days, 7 days a semaine, for a few hundred dollars a year? Mu guedzdz idz YES! Well, in dzimrle termdz, a Forex robot aldzo known adz a Forex Trading Robot idz dzimilar to a virtual stock broker. Forex robots will provide you with Forex trading advice 24/7. Thidz dzorhidztisated software will advise you on which foreign currency to buy or sell. It can monitor international markets while you sleep! These forex robots are great for people who travel a lot and need to monitor foreign markets.

They also work well for people who have little or no experience in the forex market.

You will need a computer and an internet connection to be able to use a Forex Robot (forex robot). If you are a member of a company that offers Forex Robots, you will need to pay a small fee and then you can log in 24/7 to trade online.

Chapter 2: The Advantages And Disadvantages Of Forex Trading

Forex trading can have many benefits, but there are also many pitfalls. Before you make the plunge, however. These are some of the benefits of forex trading.

Trading costs are low. Forex brokers don't charge commissions, unlike other securities traders. Instead, forex brokers make their money by the spreads between the ask price and the bid price for a trade. The "bid" refers to what you get when you sell a currency, and the "ask", is what your pay when you purchase it. The broker's earnings per trade is the difference between these two. The trade costs are already included so you don't need to separate them.

Different trading styles can be accommodated on the market. Forex trading can accommodate different trading styles. Day traders may hold their positions for just a few hours, while long-term investors might hold on for several days or even weeks.

Forex market liquidity is high. The market is very liquid due to large numbers of profit participants. Even large trades can be handled without significant price derivations. This is unlike other securities markets, where there is little chance of price manipulation or anomalies. A high liquidity market also means tighter spreads between trades which allows for more efficient pricing.

There are no capital requirements. Forex brokers offer leverage, which allows you to trade with very little capital. If your broker allows you trade with leverage up to 1:100, you can trade $100 per $1 in your trading account.

There are many currency pairs that you can trade. There are 28 currency pairs traders can trace, including EUR/USD and USD/CHF. These four pairs are the most traded on the market.

Forex market volatility is high. Forex traders have the opportunity to profit from large price swings in major currencies. There is always the possibility of big losses if the market moves against you. However, experienced traders will be able to recognize when to exit a trade in order to capture profits.

These are the disadvantages:

Forex market is opaque. Forex is not regulated by any regulatory agencies and brokers control the market. This means traders need to be aware of the risks. The broker might not offer you the best spreads for your trades or the best trading quotes. Avoid these problems by only dealing with brokers that have voluntarily agreed to be regulated and supervised by CySEC (the Cyprus Securities and Exchange Commission).

High leverage comes with high risk. Trading with leverage of 1:100 will allow you to trade with relatively low capital, but it can also significantly increase your profits. However, this also increases the risk of losing your capital.

Forex trading can be extremely technical. Forex traders need to be able to identify trading opportunities, even though currency prices are often affected by political and economic developments. Technical analysis is the process of analyzing price movements to identify patterns that could help you to find trading opportunities and places to exit or enter a trade. Although brokers offer a range of tools to help you perform technical analysis, you still need to know how to use them.

Why trade Forex?

There are many securities that you can choose from when it comes to investing. Why forex? We will be comparing currency trading with other types of trading to better understand its benefits.

Individual Blue Chip Stocks

Blue chip stocks are those issued by well-known, established companies that have a proven track record of financial soundness. Many of these companies are well-known, including Lockheed Martin and AT&T, but others are smaller names that do business in the basic sector, such as NuStar Energy L.P. and STMicroelectronics N.V. They can be traded on major stock exchanges, such as the New York Stock Exchange.

Trading forex is more speculative than trading blue-chip stocks. Traders profit from short- and medium-term price movements. They don't hold onto their positions for long periods of time.

Blue-chip stocks, on other hand, are not subject to the same price volatility that blue chip stocks do. This is absent factors like the announcement of a merger, major acquisition, or scandals such as the withdrawal of a product from the stock market. However, these stocks are not immune to problems as demonstrated by the bankruptcy of General Motors and Lehman Brothers during the 2008 global recession. Blue chip stocks can be a safe investment vehicle, especially if you're saving for retirement or long-term goals. These stocks are favored by investors because they not only provide consistent growth but also reliably pay dividends.

Individual Penny Stocks

These penny stocks have a small market capitalization, and they trade at a low price. These stocks are not traded on the major stock exchanges. They are high-risk investments due to their lack of liquidity and limited disclosure. Originally, this term was used to describe stocks trading for less than $1. However, the Securities and Exchange Commission expanded the definition to include stocks trading below $5 per share.

Penny stocks are highly speculative and are therefore ideal for investors who are open to taking high risks, but also have high potential rewards. These stocks are long-term investments, just like blue-chip stocks. Any price gains are typically seen over a longer period of time. This is because the companies that issue these stocks tend to be small businesses that are still growing. It is important to remember that penny stocks can be a promising option for companies such as tech startups. If the company grows, their value could skyrocket.

Both currencies and penny stocks can be highly speculative. However, forex trading is more straightforward. It can be difficult for companies to disclose information about penny stocks, as they do not have to file disclosures to the Securities and Exchange Commission. It is much easier to select a currency pair to trade because all of the information is easily accessible. You can also easily identify trading opportunities by analysing price movements to determine whether there are upward or downward trends.

Currency ETFs

ETFs, or currency exchange-traded funds, are being promoted as safer ways to invest in forex than trading at the spot market. A currency ETF is a collection of currencies held in a fund. Shares of the fund are then made available to the public. ETF shares can be traded on exchanges just like stock shares. ETF shares are designed to reflect the value of the currency they hold. A currency ETF holding euros, for example, is designed to reflect the currency's performance versus the US.

For traders who are interested in investing in the forex market, but do not want to trade actively, currency ETFs can be a great choice. If you want to profit from the appreciation in the US dollar relative to the UK pound, an ETF could be an option.

Trading currency ETFs has one drawback. They are shares of stock, so you must pay a commission to the broker for each transaction. These commissions can add up and eventually impact your profits. You cannot trade ETFs outside of market hours on major exchanges like forex. You cannot also trade currency ETFs without depositing additional funds into your account. There are no limits on how many times you can trade the forex spot market.

There are many options

Option is a contract that allows you to purchase or sell assets at a specific price. There are two types: call ("buy") and put ("sell") options. Binary options is a popular option trading. The trader wagers on whether or not an asset's value will rise or fall over a certain time period. You trade options because you have the ability to control a specific asset for a set period of time.

Trading options offer the advantage of making money regardless of market direction. Options that bet on market movement can be purchased. The amount you can lose is very small, as you only pay a minimal premium to get the option. You can simply let the contract end if you lose a bet. The amount you can win is also limited.

Trading options have a downside. You can only trade during hours the exchange is open. This is different from forex. It might prove difficult to schedule trading options sessions if you work a full-time job. Options markets are extremely regulated and you can trade with confidence without worrying about being cheated by your broker.

Chapter 3: Key Forex Trading Terms You Will Need To Know

Knowing the most important terms and phrases used in forex trading is one of the fastest and easiest ways to learn about it. These terms will determine how quickly or slow you can learn advanced forex trading terminology. This will allow you to accelerate your learning and help you achieve your profit-making goals. You'll take a longer path to forex trading success than if you skip this step.

Let's begin with the concept or term of pairs. Forex currencies are quoted in pairs when buying and selling, such as GBP/USD (British Pound) and JPY/MYR(Japanese Yen - Malaysian Ringgit). This is why? This is because there are always two transactions simultaneously affected by forex transactions: a buy transaction and a sale transaction. Let's start with the GBP/USD currency pair.

Let's suppose you are interested in trading the British Pound, also known as the Pound Sterling, using your U.S. Dollars, i.e. buying GBP. Let's say that the current exchange rate to buy it is $1.30. You can buy GBP and sell JSD for GBP when you purchase the GBP. This transaction involves buying British Pounds, and then selling US Dollars.

Let's suppose that the GPB buying rate rose to $1.35 per Pound Sterling after a while. It is possible to sell your GBP assets and receive more JS dollars than you had when you first started. Then, you will be able to SELL your GPB and buy back your USD. This is why currency pairs are important.

You will also need to know how forex rates are quoted in order to properly read them. The "base" currency is one of two currencies. The other, or the "quote", is the counter currency. The currency being traded is the base currency, while the counter or quote currency is used to purchase or sell the base currency.

How do you determine which currency is which? The base currency is shown on the left side of the quotation. The counter or quote currency is on the right. In our GBP/USD example above, the British Pound is the base currency and the United States Dollar is the counter or quote currency. To buy GBP you will need USD. If you wish to sell GBP, your payment will be in USD.

How do you interpret quotes for trading purposes? Prices are quoted in currency pairs. Quotes can also be presented in pairs. The ask and the bid (or "offer") price are the two most common pairs. The bid price refers to the price at the which your forex broker or counterparty will buy the base currency, while the ask price or offer price refers to the price at the which the same counterparty would sell the base currency.

Let's take the GBP/USD example and say the current bid price for the pair is $1.29, while the current offer or ask price is $1.32. This means that your broker or counterparty will buy GBP from you at $1.29 per Pound, while it is willing to sell GBP for $1.32 per Pound. If you wish to purchase GBP immediately, you will need to "hit" the forex broker or counterparty's asking price. This means that you must buy up at that price. You will need to "hit" the broker's asking price to immediately sell your GBP holdings. This is done by selling below that price. You will need to wait for your counterparty's ask and bid price to move in the right direction.

If you want to make profitable trades, you will need to be familiar with depreciation and appreciation. Appreciation is when the base currency (GBP) has appreciated in value relative to the counter or quote currency. The GBP's exchange rate went up from $1.29 to 1.32. This means that the GBP is now worth more dollars at $1.32 than it was initially at $1.29.

On the other hand, depreciation means that the base currency's value vis-a-vis its quote currency has fallen. The GBP/USD pair is our favorite. A drop in exchange rate from $1.32 - $1.29 indicates that the GBP's value has declined vis-a-vis USD.

In reverse, appreciation of one currency can mean that the value of the other currency in the pair has declined in value vis-a–vis the appreciated currency. The USD has declined vis-a-vis GBP in the recent appreciation. Instead of $1.29, USD will now cost you $1.32 per British Pound. The GBP will appreciate from $1.32 to $1.29 which means that you'll require less USD per British Pound. This means that USD has increased in value relative to GBP.

How does this translate into forex trading that can make you a lot of money? Let me explain another important principle of forex trading: positioning. You can choose from three positions in forex trading: short, long, and square. If your position in a currency is "long", it means that you have or own a certain amount of that currency. If you are "long" on GBP it means that you have a certain amount of GBP in your current account. You can also go long to buy the currency.

A short position is when you owe your broker, or another counterparty, a certain amount of a particular currency. If your GBP position is short, you owe your counterparty a certain amount of GBP. You will need to repay or deliver it at a particular time. If your position is square, it means that you don't own or owe anyone any specific amount of a currency.

How does this relate to the principle depreciation and appreciation? If you believe that one currency will appreciate in value relative to another, such as GBP/USD then you can take a profit trading position by buying GBP (or buying it) using your USD, which is at $1.29. If you believe that the currency's value will rise to $1.32, then you can sell your GPB holdings for $0.03 per Pound Sterling.

If you think that the GBP is likely to lose value relative to another currency, such as the USD, then you can sell your GBP assets now, while they are still expensive. What if you don't have any GBP holdings? How can you make a profit on the expected

USD depreciation? Short-selling the GBP can be done against the USD.

Short-selling is selling something that you don't yet own. It may seem ethical or legal to you. It's legal in certain circumstances. Is it ethical? It is ethical? This is my job, to show you how forex trading can make you money.

Let's get back to short-selling. Is it legal? Your forex broker or a friend can lend you the currency you are planning to short-sell. Referring to the GBP/USD example, if you believe the GBP will appreciate from $1.32 to £1.20 within a short time frame, and you do not have any GBP in hand, your forex broker may allow you to borrow the amount that you wish to short-sell. You can also buy the GBP you owe to your broker at a lower USD price than you received initially when you short-sold it. This can help you make a good profit.

Chapter 4: How To Start Forex Trading

Forex trading is not something you can do without much effort before exchanging currencies. To make your first trade, you must have done extensive research and performed market analysis. Here are the steps a trader must take to be able to start trading forexes successfully.

Terminology for Forex Trading

A lot of terms are unfamiliar to traders who are just beginning and have vocabularies. An aspiring trader should be familiar with these terms, and learn how to correctly use them when trading. It is essential that traders do not misunderstand certain terms when trading. New traders may find the terminology a bit confusing and they might have a different meaning from the one that was formed. These words are part of common trading vocabularies.

Pip. Pip is the lowest measurement of the currency's value under observation. However, pip is an abbreviation for the term-percentage. Pip is the lowest possible measurable value of currency movement. It always measures ad 1 percent of the currency trader wishes to exchange. In the forex market, a currency can increase or decrease by one pip. This inference means that the currency has either increased or decreased by 1pc. The market analysis tools can show that the US Dollar has increased by one pip. This means that the US dollar's value has increased by $0.0001.

This is how a pip can be inferred and its meaning. Trades are always done in terms of pip, so trader may trade with as many pips possible. Because the currency measures the smallest value, the pips represent the lowest value.

The base currency. The base currency is the currency that a trader currently holds. Your country's currency will be your base currency. The US dollar will be the base currency for a trader who is from the US. The base currency for a trader who is not from the US will be the dollar. Due to geographical differences, the base currencies of traders can differ across traders all over the world.

The asking price. The asking price refers to the amount of money your broker firm will demand or ask you to pay when you make a trade. This is the amount of money that a broker will demand from you when they accept the pair of currencies. This is the price you paid to buy the quote of the pair of currencies. It is important to note that the asking price is the price charged by brokerage firms. This is discussed below.

Bid price. Bid price. This is a reference to brokerage firms. It is the amount that brokers are willing to purchase or bid on the base currency you currently hold. Based on their ability to bid for the base currency, the broker firm determines the bid price.

Quote currency. Contrary to the base currency, the quote currency is the currency that a trader would like and be willing to buy in exchange for their base currency. The Rand is the quoted currency if a trader needs to convert US dollars into South African Rand. When the currencies are combined into pairs, it is always used to stroke against the base currency.

Spread. The spread is the commission the broker firm earns by being a forex trading platform. The spread, which can also be referred to as the spread, is the difference between the broker's bid price and the asking price. This price can also be quoted by the broker.

These are just a few of the most important terms used in forex trading. This knowledge alone is not enough. You need to be familiarized with other words and phrases related to forex trading. You won't find forex trading in only books. There are also forums, videos and other places where it is discussed.

Find the right broker firm

You will need a brokerage company that offers an online platform to open and close forex trades. It is important to find the right broker firm. Other brokers may try to scam people out of their money. A trader should do extensive research about the available brokers and choose the best. Consider the ask price and bid price of the broker, as well as other important factors such margin and leverage. A broker should provide excellent customer service, which is great for traders who are just starting out. Many broker companies offer training courses on forex trading that can be very helpful to new traders. Review by forex traders can be a good place to start when evaluating the quality of a broker.

An Analysis of the World Economy

Analyzing the global economic trends is crucial to understand the factors that could cause currencies to rise or fall in value. This will allow you to make profits and gain in the trades you make. This will help you predict the value of the currency pair that you are exchanging and whether it will be profitable or not. When evaluating the global economy, you should consider factors like the political climate in countries with strong currencies, natural factors that can influence the economy of other countries, and the Gross Domestic Product (GDP) of the country whose base currency you wish to exchange with. Other minor factors to consider include the investment rate and the investment rate. It is important to evaluate which countries are open to growth and developing opportunities when deciding the currency that will be used to trade. You can also use the analysis of the global economy to determine if the currency you are looking to buy in exchange for your base currency is performing well and set to rise in value. If the value of the quote currency increases, you can convert it into the base currency. You can find many online tools that provide information on the economic performance of various countries. You can also rank countries in terms of their GDP, which makes it easier to select the countries that will experience growth and development. It is helpful to keep up with global trends in order to gain information that can be useful in forex trading. An forex trader who is new to forex trading may sign up to several forex channels and outlets in order to stay informed about events that could affect the currency's value. This may cause the outlook for the trade to change. It is important to have the right information at all times in order to make gains and prevent loss of your money.

Opening the First Trade

Opening and closing the first trade is the process of pairing currencies. This happens when the base currency and the quote currency have been paired, and there is an appropriate trading window. A trade is an order to buy a currency in exchange for your base current. The analysis tools that brokers often offer in software programs will be available to you. Some platforms allow you to place orders immediately, while others may take a little longer. Many brokerage firms provide live prices and exchange rates for the currencies being traded. A trade might only be the first for a new trader. However, others may open up trades in a shorter time. It is best to only open a few trades so that the trader feels comfortable with trading.

Chapter 5: Hazards In Trading Foreign Currencies

Few investors are successful trading foreign currencies. Investors and traders often fail to realize the risks involved in leveraging. They take high risks and use low margins. They also want to make more money, so they trade in higher-risk areas.

Discipline when making trading decisions

Many traders are emotionally driven. When trading foreign currencies, traders often have a difficult time controlling their emotions. If a trader wants to succeed, he must be able limit his losses and maximize profits. If he loses repeatedly, he must keep his faith and patience. He must not be afraid or greedy about his trading decisions. He must be disciplined and adhere to his carefully-constructed trading plan.

Use a Trading Plan

Foreign currency traders must follow a trading plan. A person can lose sight of the goal if he fails to plan. A written trading plan is essential to help trader manage risk and maximize profits. A trader who has a strategy plan will not fall for the many pitfalls of trading.

How to adapt to foreign exchange markets

Foreign currency traders must have a plan for each type of trade even before the market opens. To minimize the risk of losing large amounts of money, he analyzes each scenario and creates a plan.

A trader can lose money even if he has a plan. However, a trader may be able to use current market conditions as a tool to improve and refine his strategies. Because he has a plan, he doesn't panic when there is an unexpected market move. He is able to learn how to adapt to foreign exchange markets, which allows him to stay ahead and make money.

Trade Foreign Currencies using Trial and Error

Trader who uses trial and error to trade foreign currencies will only lose his hard-earned cash because the practice is inefficient. Because it affects his finances, he cannot learn from his mistakes.

A new trader should seek out the guidance of experts, or find information online about foreign currency trading. A mentorship program or formal lesson can be arranged with an experienced and reputable foreign currency trader who is known for his success.

Be realistic about your expectations

An experienced foreign exchange trader will know that trading foreign currency is not going to make him rich immediately. To make long-term profits, he must be skilled. He must be able to master his strategies and not take on too much risk. Trader of foreign currencies requires discipline. He should have a plan and follow it. He must also set realistic goals.

The Right Money and Risk Management Strategies

Traders are focused on their trading and risk management strategies. He may make unprotected trades or not use stop-loss order. If he abruptly stops trading, he may not be able take advantage of the currency pair's earning potential.

A trader who wants to be successful must be able and willing to risk money. He is happy with the potential benefits that his capital will bring. He uses diversification strategies to protect his capital as his trading account grows. He has learned from experience that it is best to not expose too much capital to high-risk trades.

Managing Leverage

Foreign exchange trading can be extremely risky. This is because financial leveraging allows traders to make more money. Leveraging allows traders to increase their profits but also increases their risk. Foreign currency traders can leverage at a ratio of 400 to 1. This means that their $1 in trading volume is worth

$400. He has the potential to make a lot of money, but he also has the potential to lose a lot.

A foreign exchange trader might take advantage of the 2:1 leverage ratio to trade a standard lot worth $100,000, even though he has only $50,000 in his trading account. He can also invest in 10 10,000 mini lots using the same leveraging ratio and $50,000 of capital. He can also invest in 100 micro lots worth $1,000 with the same amount of money.

If the trader wants to leverage, the foreign currency broker will usually require that he deposit a certain amount. Margin, also known as margin, acts as an insurance policy for the broker in the event that the trader loses his money. If the trader makes a mistake in trading, the broker can demand that he deposit more money into his trading account. The broker can also allow the trader to sell any position he needs to recoup his capital. An undercapitalized trader is likely not to succeed if he leverages, even though he only has a small capital. He may be driven by greed or desire to make a lot of money with a small amount of capital. This can lead to poor trading decisions.

Leveraging can not only increase losses but also raise transaction costs. A wise trader should know the transaction costs of his broker before making his first trade. The transaction costs will be higher if the leverage ratio is high.

The foreign exchange market is more volatile than the stock market. Traders must realize that high leverage levels can cause big losses. There are also risks such as macroeconomic and political risk that can cause inefficiencies in the currency price over the short-term.

Chapter 6: Forex History And Market Participants

It is important to learn about the history of currency exchange and currencies, as well as the global nature of forex market before you enter any trades. This section will examine the history and evolution of the international monetary system. Then, we'll take a look at some of the key players in the forex market. This is something all forex traders should know.

The History of the Forex

Gold Standard System

One of the most significant events in the history forex market's history is the 1875 creation of the gold standard monetary structure. Prior to the implementation of the gold standard, international payments were made by countries using silver and gold. External supply and demand can affect the value of silver and gold as a means of payment. The discovery of a new mine for gold would, for example, drive down gold prices.

The gold standard was based on the idea that governments would guarantee the conversion of currency into a certain amount of gold and vice versa. This means that a currency would be supported by gold. To meet currency exchange demand, governments required a substantial amount of gold reserves. All major economies had established a currency equivalent to one ounce of gold in the late nineteenth century. The exchange rate between currencies was determined by the difference in the price of one ounce of gold. This was the first standardized currency exchange system in history.

The gold standard was eventually broken down at the start of World War I. The political tensions with Germany led to large-scale military projects being required by the major European powers. These projects were so costly that there wasn't enough gold available at the time for exchange.

Although the gold standard made a slight comeback in the interwar years, most countries had already dropped it by the time of World War II. But gold has never lost its ultimate value as a monetary currency. (For more information, see The Gold Standard Revisited: What is Wrong with Gold? Use Technical Analysis in The Gold Markets.

Bretton Woods System

The Allies believed there would need to be a monetary system to fill the gap left by the abandonment of the gold standard system before the end of World War II. More than 700 Allies representatives met in July 1944 at Bretton Woods (New Hampshire) to discuss what would become the Bretton Woods system for international monetary management.

For simplicity, Bretton Woods was responsible for the formation of these:

Fixed exchange rates are a method to determine the value of currency.

The U.S. dollar will replace the gold standard and become a primary reserve currency.

Three international agencies were created to monitor economic activity: the International Monetary Fund, International Bank for Reconstruction and Development and the General Agreement on Tariffs and Trade.

Bretton Woods was notable for its replacement of gold as the standard of conversion for world currencies. Further, the U.S. Dollar became the only currency to be backed by the gold. This was the main reason Bretton Woods failed.

In order to remain the reserve currency of the world, the U.S. would have to experience a series balance of payments deficits over the next 25 years. In the 1970s, U.S. gold reserve was so low that it was unable to pay all foreign central bank reserves.

On August 15, 1971, U.S. President Richard Nixon shut down the gold window and announced that the U.S. would no longer exchange gold for U.S. dollar foreign reserves. This was the end of Bretton Woods.

Although Bretton Woods did not last, the important legacy it left has an impact on today's international economy climate. The legacy can be seen in the three international agencies that were created in the 1940s, the IMF, International Bank for Reconstruction and Development (now part the World Bank), and GATT, which was the precursor to the World Trade Organization. You can read more about Bretton Wood in What Is the International Monetary Fund? and Fixed and Floating Exchange Rates.

Current Exchange Rates

The collapse of the Bretton Woods system led to the acceptance by the world of floating foreign currency rates in the 1976 Jamaica agreement. The end of the gold standard meant that floating foreign exchange rates would no longer be used. This does not mean that governments have abandoned the free-floating exchange rates system. The following exchange rate systems are still in use by most governments:

* Dollarization;

* Pegged rate

* Managed floating rate

Dollarization

This is when a country stops issuing its own currency and adopts another currency as its national currency. Dollarization is a way for a country to be considered more stable and attractive for investment. However, it has the disadvantage that its central bank cannot print money or implement any monetary policy.

Chapter 7: How To Start Trading

Education is key to currency trading success, just like any venture that has risks and rewards. An investor or investor who is successful will be distinguished from a hobbyist who plays with his own money. Currency trading is a form of betting like stock exchange. You can lose all your money or make more. To make money, not lose it, you must first understand the basics of currency trading. Then, find the right strategies to help you get out of trouble or reduce your losses. If the market turns against your.

It takes time to develop and refine business strategies. However, the purpose of this ebook was to identify strategies so that you can be at the forefront of your game, rather than someone who learns by trial and error. The latter group may not understand the importance to stick with a strategy. We are not trying to defeat a horse. Our goal is to teach you Jedi-like tricks that will allow you become a lightsaber trader on the Forex market. The best use of this lightsaber lies in understanding what it is and when to not use it. Our goal is to give Jedi spirit guidance, so you can trade lightsabers in the Forex market. The best part about this lightsaber is understanding what it is and how to use it. You are more likely to be at the forefront than someone who learns through trial and error. The latter may not understand the importance to stick with the strategy. We are not trying to defeat a horse; our goal is for you to learn Jedi-like tricks that will allow you become a lightsaber trader on the Forex market.

To give you an idea about how important it is to approach currency trading with strategy, let's say that you buy cheap and sell high. This strategy is logical and it works. The strategy is to buy currency at a low price (relatively to the US dollar), and then to sell it at a higher price or when the price goes up. This strategy is not as simple as it appears. There are many variables that could make it more complicated than it appears. One, the exchange rate change can be so small that a small purchase can result in a small sale. This can translate into a small change in the amount of thousands of dollars. It can even be less than a penny. It's also not always easy knowing when it is time to sell. What happens to your currency when it slows down? When is the best time to sell? Let's suppose you bought a euro due to the favorable exchange rate against the US dollar. The euro gained in value so it earned. But now, the euro's value is declining. What should you do? Do you want to sell now? Do you wait or will the euro rise? What are you waiting for? It is possible that you will soon realize that the euro is less valuable than you paid. Instead of buying cheap and selling high you actually bought high and then sold low. What should you do? Is it time to sell? Wait, when will the euro rise again? Wait, what are you waiting? It is possible that you will soon realize that the euro is less valuable than you paid. Instead of buying cheaply and selling high, it bought low and then sold high. What should you do? What should you do? Are you still waiting?

Forex brokers

While we place Forex brokers at the bottom on our list of things that you must have to trade, we will discuss this first item as it is crucial to understanding the other items and how to make the most of them. What is a Forex broker? You, the trader, are nothing more than an ant in a currency-game. A broker with more information will allow you to trade through them. You are not yet a Jedi, and you are not even a Jedi scholar. Professional traders will attempt to make you walk in Ermenegildo Zgna shoes for $ 1000, but you are just an ant or millipede. You don't remember what you ate for breakfast, so these guys will talk about Fibonacci analysis or mood analysis. These guys won't allow you to interact with them. Your broker, broker has access to information from interbanks about currency offers and queries. Although $

25,000 is a large sum and you have worked hard to earn it, you must understand that banks trade billions of dollars and that the amount of numbers they will manage is incomprehensible. You will deal with a broker, also known as a stockbroker, rather than directly with banks that hold money. Register in a brokerage or brokerage platform. You can then use your electronic platform for transactions. You have access to information from interbanks, including exchange offers and queries.

There are many options available when it comes to choosing a forex broker, just like any market that deals in money. While this ebook is not about choosing a forex broker, it can help you to understand the various types of brokers and their platforms. This information might be familiar to those who have been involved in currency trading. However, it may be new to many. There are many types of brokers. However, there are two main divisions: trading table brokers or trading table brokers. In the next section, we will discuss the differences. There are two types of subdivisions for agents who do not have a negotiating board or don't have one: Direct Processing (SCP), and Electronic Communication Network + Direct Processing [ECN + SCP]. This chapter is a prelude to a strategy presentation that you will use in the next chapter. Understanding the basics of currency trading is essential to understanding how transactional tables function.

Spread trading is also known as spread trading. It is basically combined buying and selling. Transaction tables work with spreads. Spreads aren't just for currency trading. They are important in all commodity futures transactions. A margin can be thought of as a combination of buying and selling one currency. An operating table operation is where you place an order for the desired operation (e.g USD-JPY) and the operating tables execute the order. Market makers are trading table brokers. They function as an independent market and not by simply combining pages. Some investors do not choose to trade through the trading table. Technically, a Dealing Desk broker could end up on the opposite side of the transaction. This means that your earnings may be inversely related to theirs.

Chapter 8: The Mechanics Of Trading

Knowledgebase

Forex is just like any other industry. To trade, you need to be familiar with the terms used by that industry. These terms are used by the industry to simplify trading and provide common measurements. You will need this knowledge base to trade Forex.

Pips

Forex traders call a pip or pips movement in Forex. A pip is a movement within the ten thousandth decimal position, or.0001. The currency pair USD/EUR is considered to have moved fifty pip when it moves from 0.93 to 99335. Pip is not complicated, but it is a symbol of the price shifts in currency pairs. These currencies move in small increments, and it is worth noting that the pip is the most important decimal place. Although currencies fluctuate at lower rates than a Pip and sometimes several thousand higher than a Pip, the pip is still the most basic measurement we have for an individual currency pair.

You will see changes in currency pairs measured in pips. This metric is not only useful, but it can also be used to determine your profitability and minus broker fees. Let's say that the USD/EUR trades at 1.1 Then, there is an increase of 27 pip, or a change to 1.1027. In this example, the US Dollar gained in value. To calculate your profit from this 27-pip move, simply multiply your total investment and subtract the conversion rate for pips. This is 1000 *.0001 = 1,000 USD if you have invested $1,000 USD in US currency. Divide this number by the currency trading rates of the currency pair. 1/1.1027 = 1.91 This number represents the dollar per pip profit ratio. Now multiply this number by the number pips.91 x 27 = 24.57. With a fluctuation rate of 27 pips and this investment, you will have $24.57.

A note: While the pip refers generally to the fourth place in all currencies, it is not the case with Asian currencies. The pip is only the second place in Asian currencies. One pip is 0.01 for the Japanese Yen. This is due to the way these currencies are ranked. These currencies don't use decimal places but have multiplied everything by 100 to get relative prices. It makes sense that pips are moved between two decimal places. This is important to remember when considering Asian currencies. It can be confusing if you don't understand how pips in these markets are measured.

Stop-Loss Orders

Stop loss orders can be a great tool for traders. Even if you don't have access to the broker's specific tools, it can still be helpful to set up mental stops for yourself. Stop-loss orders are lower bounds that you can use to exit a trade. Your broker can issue an order stating that if a currency pair hits a certain price, you must sell all your holdings. Stop-loss orders do exactly what they sound to prevent you from losing more money on the market. These orders are especially useful for value traders who don't monitor their holdings regularly, as well as day traders who trade with multiple currency pairs and have different investments at once.

Even if you don t have a broker to set up a stop-loss order, it is important that you set up a mental stop loss. You should find a price point at which you are no longer comfortable investing. This was my saving grace in trades that didn't go well and also when I wasn't sure if it was worth staying committed. Being a successful trader requires you to overcome fear and hold firm to your convictions. It is difficult to decide when you should withdraw from a trade when real money is at stake. Stop-loss orders remove a lot of stress as you make a decision without your money at risk. This allows you to consider the risks in a rational way. Percentage-based is the way I prefer to calculate maximum losses. If I invest $100, my maximum loss is 20 percent. If I'm monitoring an investment, I have a mental stop-loss order. I also place a physical stop loss order with my broker if it is long-term or value trades. In the early stages and months of trading, it is important to know your limits and use this feature provided by your broker.

Currency Pairs

Chapter one showed you how money can be made by the exchange of currencies and the passing of time. You saw, in particular, the conversion of US dollars into Euros and back again. This is an example a currency pair. You are always purchasing into a particular currency pair when you buy into a currency. You pay a base amount in US dollars to purchase a pair. Don't worry about finding the right currency pair for you. Currency pairs are a dynamic relationship between countries. The currency pair reflects the country's purchasing power. Chapter 1 focuses on the Euro. The decline in the US Dollar's value has resulted in European nations gaining purchasing power over American goods. This dynamic relationship can be useful for investors and businesses other than Forex markets.

You can think of currency pairs as either standard or exotic pairs. Exotic pairs fluctuate at a higher rate and/or have smaller volumes. Because you have a smaller investor pool, exotic currency pairs can be more risky to trade. You don't have the same level of information and clarity that you get from trading larger currency pairs. You may also have difficulties selling a currency at the right time. Volatility changes in exotic currency pairs can be explained by one or both of the currencies in the pair. The more volatile a currency is due to external influences, the smaller the economy. Also, trades with fewer traders are more important in changing its value. USD/NOK and USD/DNK are two examples of exotic currency pairs. This is the US dollar being pegged against the Danish

Kroner or Norwegian Kroner. Although you might not consider Norway and Denmark to be volatile, this is not what makes an exotic pair. This is important to remember when looking at currency pairs. It isn't always easy to tell which pair is standard and which is exotic. However, some brokers will label currency pairs accordingly.

Spread

You are not purchasing USD directly from the US government if you buy USD on a Forex exchange. You are not buying the currency outright, but you are purchasing it from another trader. It is easy to see that the trading value for a currency may not be the real value you will receive. The trading value of a currency is only indicative of the average of several trades or, in certain cases, the most recent trade. You are purchasing currency from traders just like you. They want to make the most money possible. Spread is the difference between the asking and the bid prices of currencies. It helps buyers and sellers to meet. Imagine a currency pair trading at 1.21. This would mean that you would get 1.21 * the value of the base currency on an exchange. This currency may not be available for trading at 1.2099 or something higher depending on demand. The spread is the difference between the price you will pay and the offer made by the seller. The spread in this instance is 0.001, which is ten pips.

Spread is an indicator of the direction a currency is headed in. This is why it is important to remember. Spreads widening make it more difficult to purchase or sell currency pairs. However, spreads narrowing mean that the currency is much more liquid. Spread increases usually indicate that there is a reversal or that the currency value will slow down. Spreads can be used to forecast future currency values and to help you decide when it is best to sell your currency. Volume is not an issue for standard currency pairs. However, spreads can affect your ability sell your holdings. The currency pairs you trade will determine how much spread can affect your ability to trade. You are better off trading established currency pairs as beginners to avoid volatility.

Candlestick

The candlestick is an essential graph for studying the history of currency pairs' prices. A candlestick is a line graph that displays the price fluctuation. Y represents the price and time. Unique is the way each data point is presented.

Although the graph above may appear confusing, it actually displays a lot of information in the most simple way. The simple X axis is time, and the Y as price. The data points are made from candlesticks. The filled blocks indicate a decline in price and the hollow white blocks indicate an increase in price. This is the core of candlesticks' operation. By looking at this information about each data point you can see where each data point stands in relation to other data points. It is a change or decrease in the blink of an eye. This allows you to measure currency pairs at different times to see different effects. This graph can be displayed on a daily, weekly, or yearly basis. Each data point could represent the month and day, hour, minute, hour, and minute. The currency pair is measured in units of time. These candlesticks are the unit of time. You will also see a bar extending from the top and bottom. This indicates the magnitude of the change. A tall bar at its top signifies a positive change while a shorter bar at its bottom is indicative of a decrease. The length of the bar's body shows volatility in currency prices. Longer blocks indicate more volatility. This will be your primary metric if you use primarily analytical strategies. You will thrive on volatility.

Reading a Currency Pairs Graph

A currency pair can only be defined as one ratio. It can be hard to see how a currency pairing ratio affects the whole currency pair when you're just starting out. The current exchange rate for the NZD/USD or

New Zealand Dollar/US dollars pair is 0.73. If you have US dollars and you want to make profits, you'd want this rate to drop. This would be a line that has a slope of 0. It is best to hold the first currency pair if it is moving upwards. If it is moving downwards, it is best to keep the second currency pair. Although this may seem simple, many people don't know how to interpret these graphs correctly. People are so used to seeing growth and the line charts going up that they often forget that it is not in their best interests. This is a side effect of the single ratio not always being intuitive in finding positive directions for a single currency. I have seen it happen to smart people before.

Currencies: Options

Do not trade currencies options - this should only be done by more experienced traders. Options markets for currencies can provide some valuable information. Let me briefly explain what the different types of options are and how they work. There are call options and put choices.

Each is the opposite of the other. You can bet that the currency value will rise by using a call option. You can also bet that a currency's value will decrease by using a put option. If there are many calls on a currency in the options market, that means that many options traders believe that it will rise in value. A lot of put options is an indication that traders think a currency's value will fall.

These options allow the buyer to choose whether they want to sell or buy currency at a specific price. A call option allows me to bet that a currency's value will rise so I pay a price to purchase a contract that allows my to buy a currency pair at a lower price if it reaches a specific price by a particular date. If I have USD/EUR invested and expect the US Dollar's value to rise, I will pay for a contract that allows me to buy USD at today's price if USD trades at X date. The contract becomes worthless if USD does not reach that price by the end of that date. If the price is met then I can purchase USD at a low price and sell it immediately. The opposite is true for put options. If I want USD to fall in value, I would buy a contract that states USD will reach X price by a specific date. If USD falls to the pre-arranged price, I can purchase USD at a price specified in the contract and then immediately sell it. It will be specified in the contract that I can purchase it at a price lower than the currency market value. This ensures that I am able to make money immediately.

Because options are useful for analysing the market and also to see where options traders make their profits, I wanted to briefly explain them. Options traders are simply sellers of options. They only make money if a contract is not executed. This should serve as a strong deterrent for options traders to start trading. Early traders will purchase options based on their contract price. However, they don't realize that the chances of the contract being implemented are very low, even though it was well priced. Do not buy options. However, pay attention to the number of put and call options for a currency pair.

Price Action

Price action simply refers to the performance of a currency pair in trading. The price action can be described as the currency's'swings', positive or negative. It simply describes the trending price movement of a currency pair.

Market Hours

Forex trading has the advantage of being able to trade at any hour of the day and night. There are many markets that are open 24 hours a day. The following list will show you which exchanges are open when. The listed times are in standard Eastern Time. Adjust for your local time zone. Note that not all exchanges sell the same currency pairs. Some exchanges may sell only certain currency pairs. These exchanges have different volumes from one country to the next. For example, Sydney has a higher volume than New York's exchange.

New York, 8AM-5PM EST

Tokyo, 7PM-4AM EST

Sydney: 5PM - 2AMEST

London, 3AM-12PM EST

Chapter 9: The Daily Trend And 4 Hours

The Forex technology has made trading easier in many ways. Trading with strategies has been made easier by the 4 hour and daily trends. Websites can display charts with the daily and 4-hour trends.

When you're ready to trade, don't consider this chart as the gospel of currency pair movements. You should consider the chart as a single indicator. The chart should only be used to show you the history of a currency pair. It is important to first assess the daily and 4-hour means of the chart before discussing how to use it as an indicator.

Trend for Four Hours

A currency pair's four-hour trend can be either up or down. If the chart shows EUR/USD: Up it means that the EUR/USD has been trending up for the past four hours, depending on when the currency pair opened. If the currency pair opened at 1.1456 and has been open for four hours, it could have risen to 1.1457 or stayed there without moving. This is unlikely. It is possible that the price went up to 1.1467 and then fell back to 1.1457 before rising to 1.1477. The trend is overall up, even though the price went down slightly, it continued to rise, increasing at a faster rate each time.

The Daily Trend

The daily trend may be opposite to the 4-hour trend. Let's take for example, that the EUR/USD opened in Asia at 1.1377, and it closed four hours later at 1.1477. The daily trend has been up and the 4-hour trend up since the opening of the market during the last 4 hours.

In the last four hours, the AUD/USD price has moved from 0.0.4000 to 0.4050. However, the opening price at the start of the day was 0.0.4100. The 4-hour trend showed that the price rose, but the trend for the day was actually declining based on the opening prices. Even though the trend was up for the past four hours, the daily trend could actually indicate a decline.

What is the importance of this?

It is important that the trend matches the trading timeframe. You may be able to see the trend for the next hour if you trade within the next four hours. If this happens, the pattern will remain the same. You could, however, buy into the uptrend and expect a higher price, losing everything you invested.

How to trade on the Daily Trends and 4-hour Trends

Trades should be based on the current day. To determine the best strategy, you need to look at the entire day since Asia opened. You will need to determine if there is a clear uptrend or downtrend for the day.

To determine if the daily trend is changing, you need to compare the current trend with the daily trend. This will allow you to return to earlier chapters about other trading trends.

You might, for example, look out for indicators that indicate a major reversal trend. These indicators may not be visible, but if you do see them, you might feel confident that the daily trend will continue throughout the day or even into the next day.

If you see the indicators of a trend reversal, you can be more certain that the 4-hour trend has reverted and that the daily trend will turn upwards, possibly into the next day.

Knowing exactly what has happened is the only way to feel confident about your entry and exit points.

You can even say you want to see the weekly trend before you look at the daily and 24-hour trends.

You might want to look at the whole week's trading trends to see if the current trend is the steady trend or if it is a short reverse. If the week has been up consistently, then the downtrend on the day may be a brief reversal to lower values, before a new 52 weeks high is reached.

You can learn more about the trend and the indicators to help you understand it better.

Chapter 10: How To Choose A Forex Broker

It is important to choose a reliable Forex broker. Refco was the company that opened my first account ten years ago. It was a well-known name back then. Their services were available to anyone who wanted to trade different securities, currencies or options. The company eventually went bankrupt, causing great problems for clients. Many people's assets and accounts were frozen, and they couldn't withdraw their money for several months. Refco handed customers to FXCM, its' daughter company. This allowed people to get their money back and trade it through FXCM. Recent events in SNB saw the Bank of Switzerland remove the ceiling in EUR/chf, causing Swiss Francs to rise thousands of pips within a matter of seconds. Many brokers were also in the same position Refco was in a decade ago due to this event. Others may experience bankruptcy soon, but some went bankrupt. Any trader new to the market should carefully consider which broker he would like to work with. Let's take a look at some key points that will assist you in choosing the best broker on the market.

Avoid dealing with companies who have had legal problems in the past

It is important to verify that the company you are considering opening an account with doesn't have any problems with financial regulators. Refco, which I already mentioned, had to deal with CFTC (both regulators), on more than 100 occasions. This was something I didn't know and it cost me money. You can avoid the same fate as me by checking that the broker you are interested is registered with the regulators.

Make sure that your broker is licensed

It may surprise you to learn that many brokers are not regulated. These brokers either use loopholes in local laws, or they are offshore companies that could disappear with your hard-earned money at any moment. You can search for "unregulated Forex broker lists" to find the most up-to-date list of companies that have not been regulated by authorities. They simply act according to their own judgement before getting into trouble with regulators, customers or local authorities. To prevent your broker from doing anything illegal with your money, you need to make sure that there is a legal authority watching over him.

Look for a broker with lower spreads

It's natural to do so, right? You have better spreads but the broker also has better dealing banks that provide liquidity. This could also indicate that the broker does not play against customers, and takes their money. Your broker should have better quotes from large banks. This would indicate that they trust you and your broker.

Take into account the leverage offered

Brokers encourage high leverage, often against their customers. It is promoted as a good thing. However, you need to know how to use it properly and avoid taking too much risk. Your account can be destroyed by too much leverage in no time. Brokers that offer leverage 1:1000 or more would be a bad idea. Maximum leverage you can use should not exceed 1:100, or even better 1:50. Anything beyond this is excessive. Brokers who care about long-term clients are not looking for people who take too much risk and lose money quickly. Good brokers will not only advise you about how to reduce your risk but also take care of your spreads.

You can open an account by making a small deposit

Although this does not necessarily mean that a broker will be good at trading, a mini account can help you prepare to trade with real money without taking too much risk. A demo account doesn't prepare you for trading live. If you are willing to risk 200 or 300 dollars and you don't have the money you can afford to lose, you can open a mini trading account. You will be able trade much more effectively than with a demo account.

See customer reviews

Despite not being 100% reliable, you will still find truth to them. Avoid brokers with bad reviews. You can do more research on the opinions of clients and get a better idea about which brokers are reliable.

Are they concerned about their customers?

Many brokers offer customer service. Avoid brokers who do not offer customer service. Avoid brokers who do not respond to customer inquiries within 24 hours. One time I had to wait over a week for a response from a broker support line. This is definitely not the broker I would recommend. No. You can visit a broker website and use live chat to ask questions. Don't be afraid to ask tough questions. Be smart, it is your money at stake.

Hopefully you can see the number of points that have been covered. You will likely have other issues that you want to look into after you've reviewed all the points. It's better to be safe than sorry. You can also make a good broker part of your journey towards being a successful trader.

Take your trading to the next level by creating your own trading rules

Trading rules and discipline are probably the most important things you need in your trading toolkit. Without direction, you cannot expect to sail around the market like a ship. It is essential to understand what you are doing, and why. You will soon be eaten by market forces. Forex is a zero-sum game. To win, you must lose. You can swap the parts. You must lose in order to make someone win. You choose which part of the trade you want to make. You must create your own trading rules if you want to win. Let's take a look at some of them. You may have heard some of them as slogans. Others might be new to your ears. They will be there for you.

Cut your losses short

This is something that newbies rarely do. They expect that the trade will return and they will make a profit. They may lose half or all of their account, although it often happens. Don't give in to wishful thinking. Reduce your losses if they are small. If your trade isn't going as planned, that means something is wrong. The smartest thing is to exit the market as soon as possible. Trades should not exceed 2 percent of your account.

Profits are yours

The opposite happens to newbies. They allow their losses to run wild and reduce their profits. They lose it all. You can only increase your trading account by making more profits and losing less. You will quickly lose 200 pips if you trade 100 pips. To be successful, you must make at least twice what you lose. Trading is difficult. If you are willing to take a few pips to get ahead, but allow your losses to grow to hundreds of pip you'll be done sooner than you think. Smart traders don't let their profits run. They spot a trend and keep their positions until they have outgrown their losses by three, four, or ten times. This is how you can make money in currencies.

You can increase your exposure when you're doing well, and decrease it when you fail.

You can be more in touch with the market if you're doing well. This will increase your profits. If you're not making money, it is important to reduce your exposure to the market. If you are losing trades a lot, trade less. When you trade, you need to be able to think clearly and have stable emotions. If you feel tired or unsure of the direction of the market, don't trade. Trades are not necessary. It is important to only take advantage of opportunities you see and not those you don't. Losses can put you in a mental state that makes it difficult to recover your losses. This is a dangerous thing. This is a sure-fire way to fail. Let your head rest and then only trade.

Don't overtrade. Choose your trades

New traders often overtrade. Because they fear missing good trades, they feel the need to constantly be on the market. They end up making a lot of poor trades and losing a lot of money. You must be selective if you want to make consistent money as a trader. Random trades can lead to poor results at best, and large losses in the majority of cases.

Do not resist a trend

Most professional Forex traders know the old saying, "Trend is your friend". They trade in the direction and against the trend. You make money when you follow the market flow and not the other direction. Many newbies rely on indicators to tell them if the market is too hot or too cold. Then they begin fighting against a trend. Markets can remain in overbought and oversold territory for long periods of time when there are trends. Don't rely on these indicators. Follow it. Trend trading is the most lucrative and easy trading method. It can help you make money.

Keep an eye out for fundamental news releases

One macroeconomic news release can make a currency pair move hundreds of pips within a matter of seconds. It is not a good idea to have an open position during market events. Many pros close their positions prior to important news releases such as interest rate decision, non-farm payrolls, CPI and General Domestic Product. Always check the Economic calendar before a week begins to see what pieces of news will be coming. Do not trade during these events. Only after volatility has returned to normal levels, can you look at the Economic Calendar.

Market discounts information

Market participants are always looking forward, traders know. They anticipate things to happen. Market participants have already priced in any new information, so the market could move in the opposite direction it should. Let's suppose that the market believes the FED will raise interest rate within half a year and that the ECB will maintain them at the same level. This expectation causes the eur/usd to fall until finally, the FED raises rates. The market will likely sell the US dollar when it learns that interest rates are increasing. This is because the market has already priced this information in.

Have a trading diary

Learn from both your bad and good trades. Trading is not easy for those who don't know what to do. They keep making the same mistakes, which eventually leads them to lose all their capital. Keep track of your trades and post a chart in your journal with a description of why you opened the trade. Give a description of the trade and an explanation. Are you following your trading rules, or did you break them? You might be able to find the reason it didn't work. This practice should be done every day, and even if you don't trade as often as usual, at most once per week. You'll see the difference in your trades and how much you can learn from them.

Learn from others

Learn. Learn from successful traders and read books on financial markets and trading strategies. You will be able to become a better trader if you take their advice. Understanding how traders think, motivate themselves, analyze markets, and how they do it all is essential. These traits can be modeled and you will eventually be able to join the ranks of currency traders who consistently make money.

Chapter 11: Forex Trading Benefits

Forex can be used for currency trading or foreign exchange. It is a highly liquid, global economy that allows for large amounts of periodic trade. Forex trading, like many other acquisitions, is not for the faint-hearted or inexperienced trader.

Forex trading has been a popular option for many years, but there have been many changes to stock trading and shares trading. Forex trading overstocks has many advantages, including the large earnings potential without any restrictions. Forex trading is a 24 hour business, which means that even small investors can reap the benefits of this great opportunity. This means you can trade Forex while you are doing other things. You can even work on it at night if you wish! There is always a bank that can trade anywhere on the planet.

Forex trading is easy to learn for beginners. Forex trading fees are typically lower than for trading stocks, and you can practice marginally. You can buy large amounts of currency with a small payment. However, this comes with both risks and benefits.

Due to the fact that all operations require money, Forex trading is usually extremely fast. You'll quickly learn how to make accurate projections when you begin trading Forex. This is possible because it is easier to learn about the major currencies than the intricacies of the stock market.

These are just a few of the many benefits of Forex trading. Many of these advantages make Forex trading a great option for beginners with little investment knowledge.

You may be able to make the right decision about where you want to trade Forex.

Forex brokers are usually the ones who facilitate internet Forex trading. A broker who offers currency pairs that traders can buy and distribute online is called an online trading platform. The choice of broker is a matter of confidence. Before choosing the right broker for you, the traders must gather information about them. Traders have one concern: how much cash they spend. They worry about where their cash is going and are willing to borrow money from brokers to help them. This is why it is important to collect broker data and learn about cash laws. Information is usually found on their blog or on the Internet. This allows traders to interact with individual brokers.

This section focuses on the advantages of online Forex trading.

Market Hours

Because the country is the competition, the business can be reached 24 hours a days, 7 days a week. The industry can be divided into four segments: New York City, London, Sidney and Tokyo. They are open at different times throughout the day; that means that the New York market will close when the London market closes; the Tokyo market will close when the New York marketplace closes. The Sydney market will then open one hour later. The Tokyo market will close one hour earlier than Sidney's; the London market will reopen once Sidney has closed.

Leverage

Brokers can give traders power. This means traders who have a small amount of cash can trade with larger amounts. A broker can offer traders a 50 to 1 leverage so that they trade for 50 percent more than their actual income. A trader who has 200 euros and is trading at a 50-to-1 leverage will have a currency quantity of 10,000 Euros, or 50x200 Euros.

Low transaction costs

The rates include transaction costs and brokers may charge a small transaction fee or none at all. This is the spreading rate between selling and buying. For example, the most traded currency pair is euro/USD. Some brokers split it at 2 pips. This means that traders must earn at least 2 pips to make a EUR/USD trade profitable. The spread for the GBP/USD currency pair is another example. There are many brokers that have it set at 4 pips. This means that traders need to earn 4 pip before they can make a profit on a GBP/USD trade. The data shows that EUR/USD is the most traded currency pair because of its currency pair-based allocation.

Access

Forex traders have access to the market 24/5 (24 hour a days, 5 day a week). This gives them more business opportunities than future trades, which usually only allow for seven hours per day. Forex traders don't have to wait for the market open the next day. They can trade immediately, which makes the market more liquid and closer to cash. The forex market is also growing rapidly. Cash exchange on a weekly basis is significantly higher than that of futures.

No trading commission

Futures traders must send their broker a brokerage premium or committee for any future transactions. Forex does not have trade orders. Spreading (the difference between the current cost of an offer and the request) is how Forex brokers make cash.

Forex trading is done not only in one location but also via the internet and networks. It can be carried out in several important trading centers all over the world. Foreign exchange brokers work from their desks using a microphone connected to a telephone line. The voice of the broker is constantly transmitted to the company's voices. Forexvoice will help you understand how this works. Brokers will also assist with tender rates and bidding. You can find a list of currencies in combination such as EUR/USD. Forex trading means that you can purchase one currency and distribute another simultaneously. On the right, you will see the selling citation. This is the maximum amount that you can purchase. Also known as the bidding price of the market maker, the selling citation can also be called the bidding cost.

Forex is Very Liquid

Forex is distinctive because of the large number of foreign exchange traders and their diversity. Forex currency foundations can be affected by many variables. They are more susceptible to speculation than any other financial markets. Although the Forex market is not as profitable as other fixed-income countries, it has significant trading volumes that allow for substantial earnings.

Forex Trading Times and Geographical Dispersion are Unique

Trades can be done for nearly 24 hours per day between Monday and Friday at 17:00 EST. Trades can be made when it is easy for traders. Auto-trading can be used on many trading platforms.

A key regulatory authority is absent from the Forex industry.

Some countries have retailers that are regulated. Only deal with authorized retailers. You may find yourself in a situation where your distributor has taken your deposit.

Forex offers the chance to trade leverages, which can lead to increased profit or loss.

Margin can be used to achieve a 2:1 yield in the inventory market, while it is possible to leverage the Forex market 100:1 or 500%.

You can open a trading account starting with $25

Register your demo file with any broker or dealer, and you won't be charged a fee.

Chapter 12: Managing Expectations

Before you start your Forex trading journey, it is important to remember that this is not a quick-and-easy business. This is not a job that will make you a lot of money. Except if you're managing large sums of money like fund managers or hedge funds, this is unlikely to happen. Even then, there are many risks and even large capitals could lose a lot in the Forex market. Forex traders can make steady and decent profits if they have a system in place and some luck. An average trader will earn a return of 1 to 2 percent per month. A 25% annual return is possible. This will only occur if market conditions are favorable, and there aren't any other unforeseen events, such as war or political upheavals.

These figures show that a person who invests approximately US$100,000. in the Forex market can expect a return of about

US$25,000 per year. Although this is a substantial amount of money, most people will not choose to make Forex trading their full-time occupation. Data has shown that only 25% of retail Forex traders make any profit within three months. The majority of these traders are day traders. Others only hold a few positions and trade for longer periods.

In currency pairs, movements are often very small and only last for a few days. These currency pairs usually fluctuate by approximately 10 percent each year. The Forex market is often viewed as gambling. Forex traders argue that the odds of winning are better than any other casino game. This type of analyzed betting is a huge advantage for traders as they have lots of data and clues to help them make informed decisions. People may make bad bets, just like traditional gambling. There will be days when you can't win, no matter how rigorous your trading and analysis are. One out of three trades will result in a loss on average. Depending on your luck, it could be even worse.

It is possible to make modest amounts of money in Forex markets if you put in the effort and are focused on your charts and strategies. Once you have gotten a clear understanding of Forex expectations, it is possible to be a successful trader if one is truly committed to the endeavor. If you believe that Forex expectations are the problem, then you need to find ways to overcome them. Let's dive deeper into managing expectations when Forex trading.

Are you aware of the importance of managing Forex expectations? As I said, if you don't know your Forex expectations, you will be one of those traders who gives up before you even start trading. You must manage your Forex expectations. What are your expectations? Let's face it, expectations are impossible to ignore. Everything in this world is built on expectations. Even the most successful Forex trader will have some expectations when they enter the market. The important thing is how you dealt with market expectations. You will lose the game if you allow your expectations to play the game. Setting reasonable expectations is essential. To get a clear picture of the factors that can impact your expectations, you must first consider them.

Your expectations are influenced by your emotions. It fee s great to set reasonable expectations and get the chance to meet them. How does this relate to trading? The ability to avoid pain is a fundamental human trait. It is a natural ability that we have. Your pain-avoidance ability is different in trading. It links with emotions. You avoid any information that could invalidate your trading expectation when you create a trading expectation. You find reasons to avoid the information, rationalize them, and, worse, you feel good about it. This is not healthy. This could lead to a loss of your entire trading account.

However, you will face problems if your expectations are not managed. What happens if you have unrealistic expectations about trading? While it is perfectly acceptable to have expectations when trading, unrealistic expectations are a problem. Naive traders tend to have unrealistic expectations due to their lack of knowledge of the market. Expectations can lead to disappointments when things don't go as planned. If you feel constantly defeated and your expectations don't come true, frustration can turn into resentment toward the Forex market. You may even give up trading!

This is what happens when you expect a losing trade will turn into a profitable one. You might overlook all signals and details that support your expectations, even if the price action isn't in your favor. Because you aren't willing to accept the obvious pattern, it will be hard to see. If you are looking to continue trading in Forex markets, this is a bad sign. If you want to stay in the Forex market, you must be able to manage your expectations. You will be able to recognize the price action signals to you if you are able to manage your expectations. Sometimes you have to let the market move a bit in order to make a profit. Adjusting your expectations is the best thing you can do.

You can let go of the market if it's not manageable, but you should still manage your expectations as it is within your control. This will allow you to make rational trading decisions. Only rational decisions can help you reach your goals. It's better to explain how important it is to manage your expectations when Forex trading.

Forex trading is a complex business. It is possible that you will need to know a lot about the market before you can start trading. You should keep up to date with market news, have a plan, a journal and trading strategies. Your expectations are the foundation of your success. Forex trading requires you to anticipate market movements before you can make a decision and execute your plan. You must not make emotional decisions when trading Forex. Instead, you should be rational.

You must view emotions as your enemy if you want to trade like professionals. When you see a profitable trade signal, your emotions won't stop you from moving forward. They might even push you out of trade, even if the price signal proves profitable. Your emotions can make you a poor trader and cause you to make bad decisions. It is crucial to trade logically and not emotionally.

Emotional discipline is also important in the Forex journey. This stage is common for professional traders. Although you cannot avoid emotions or expectations, it is possible to manage your emotions and control your expectations.

Expectations are normal because we humans expect them. As I said before, expectations must be managed. You will be the one who is frustrated if you have unrealistic expectations. You will not make any profits by yourself; it is going to be a rollercoaster ride. There will be losses, so learn how to deal with them. You should not expect to win. Instead, you should give up and admit that this isn't going to be a profitable outcome. You'll be a lot more successful if you can cut down on losses and make small profits.

Chapter 13: Forex And Compound Interest

Earning more is earning more. It is common to believe that others should pay you more if you want to make more money. However, this is not always true. You can make more even if you pay yourself more than the other.

This fundamental principle underlies financial success. It was first revealed by George Samuel Clason in 1926 in his book The Richest Man In Babylon. A great motivational classic.

This principle says that a portion of your earnings must be kept. You can multiply the amount you save by putting aside 10% of your earnings. This money will not be available for ordinary expenses or extraordinary expenses. The power of compound investment can make any investment more valuable. Many people can make more money and increase their wealth by investing in themselves first. This principle is just as effective today as it was back in 1926.

Despite the fact that this 10% formula is simple, many people don't want to hear it or apply it. You are looking for quick ways to make money, but you don't have a long-term plan. A long-term investment plan, on the other hand is a solid foundation for economic stability. You can earn more by starting to pay yourself first. Your financial success will be faster if you get started early.

The Power Of Compound Interest

You can earn more by taking advantage of compound interest. This is how it works: If you invest EUR1,000 at EUR5 per annum, you will receive EUR50 in interest. At the end of the first calendar year, your total investment will be EUR1,050. You will get a 5% interest in the second year if you take out the initial investment as well as the interest earned on your current account. This is EUR52.50. You will receive 5% on

1,102.50 the third year and so forth. This rate will allow you to make your money grow in a period of 15-30 years, which is well beyond the initial investment. How much will the capital you have invested grow? It was explained by Luca Pacioli, an Italian mathematician. Capital doubles within 72 years divided by the interest rate. Let's return to the example. If the interest rate is 5% per annum, we divide 72 times 5 which gives us 14.4. This means that the initial capital doubles in 14 years and four months. As you have more time to allow the powerful magic of the interest you are able to capitalize on, the better the result. Even if you don't have a lot of money, it is worth saving now and investing in your future. There is no need to have a large sum of money. You don't need to start with a large amount of money and build it over time.

How to Pay For Yourself First

You can earn more money by paying your self first. Savings and investment should be a key part of your financial management. You can start to save a fixed amount (at least 10%) each month and invest it in a savings account you don't touch. This step should be automated, like a fixed monthly deduction from your paycheck. You won't have to depend on your self-discipline, and your ability to save money will not be affected by domestic emergencies or other circumstances. Keep increasing your savings until you are able to save enough money to invest in bonds, mutual funds or real estate. Renting is a waste of money. Your investments will build up your assets and you can live with the money that remains after you've paid yourself. Spending is a choice. You should earn more money to be able to spend. You should not use your savings to fund a more extravagant lifestyle. Your investments should grow to the point that you can live comfortably with interest if needed. Only then can you truly be financially independent and self-sufficient.

You must create assets and not liabilities if you want to make more. Instead of spending your money on someone else's wealth, invest in assets that generate other income such as stocks, bonds, real property, and gold. When your money begins to grow, you should learn more about how to invest it. Keep up-to-date with investment news and make sure you have a good policy to insure your assets. Don't blindly trust someone to manage your money. Instead, learn as much as you can about financial education. You will be financially ready to make it big. Money will come to you once this is understood.

What is compound interest? This question may not be answered by everyone. While everyone may know the basic interest (the one that withdraws at each agreed time unit), few people are able to explain the compound interest, its workings, and how to benefit from it.

It is instructive to look at a bank account as an example.

If I have a net rate at 1% on my account on January 1, I will have EUR101 by the end of the year. If the conditions remain the same, I will have EUR102 instead of EUR102. A cent is added to the capital. The cent represents 1% of the total euro that was accumulated in the previous year.

Although the basics are clear so far, most people cannot calculate compound interest and treat it as simple interest. Because of its slow start, which is especially true for small capital, it tends to be considered "irrelevant". Investors can do nothing wrong.

For example, if my capital of EUR100 has been invested for 5 years, it is now EUR140. We are led to believe that the annual interest rate was 8%.

This is because we don't take into consideration that the interest accumulates has gone to increase capital. We would have 5 years if the interest rate had been 8%.

Initial capital: EUR100

* First year: EUR108

* 2nd Year: EUR116.64

* Third year: EUR125.97

* 4th Year: EUR136.04

* 5th Year: EUR146.93

The difference of EUR6.93 is almost 7%. It is easy to get dazzled (or worse, "suffer" if we are given a simple interest for compound interest).

Simple example: The math behind compound interest

Let's say we have an initial capital in the amount of EUR1,000. The capital yields a Y% annual interest.

What is the expected return on investment in X years?

Here's how to calculate:

(1) IV = CP (1 + Y) ^ X

IV represents the return on investment after X years and CP the initial capital. Y can be expressed as a percentage. 0.04 is

4%. The symbol stands for elevation to power.

Inverse calculations tend to show that the Y interest on an investment, net of inflation, is equal to IV compared with a CP capital invested X times (years) back. Here's the formula:

(2) Y = (1 / 1 / IV / CP).

Imagine that EUR1,000 that you invested five years ago is now worth EUR1,400. This would indicate that the yield was 6.96%.

Let's look at another example.

Marie just received her salary, and now she can finally purchase the air conditioner that she needs.

Julie, her friend, calls to inform her of an urgent need she has and asks for EUR1,000.

Marie is still undecided as this would require her to wait another month before she can purchase.

The two girls agreed to a loan, provided Julie pays Mary a 5% interest.

Marie is more likely to delay her purchase if Marie does this.

Julie will be repaid EUR1,050 for the amount she borrowed instead of EUR1,000 when she returns it.

Marie will then be able to buy the air conditioner the following month and use the accumulated interest (EUR50), to go out for dinner with her boyfriend.

It was, in short, a positive recognition of delayed usage!

We now have a better understanding of the rate and how it works.

This allows us to divide the interest rate into two main categories.

Simple interest

The compound interest

Simple Interest

Let's return to the first example.

Julie pays Mary the money and the interest at the end of each period. The girl requests the same amount to purchase a new refrigerator.

Marie agrees that she will lend the money to her friend.

Julie secured her debts and new interests for EUR1,050 the following month.

Marie now has her initial capital plus EUR100 interest for a total amount of EUR1,100.

When interest is no longer earning any interest, it is considered simple.

In this example, the EUR50 first loan was not increased to the capital loaned second time.

Compounded Interest:

Changes in scenery

Marie is asked by Julie to lend her EUR1,000 and she promises to return them within two years.

Mary is open to the idea, provided Julie agrees to pay compound interest on the matured capital.

Julie will be able to add EUR 50 interest to the capital. This will increase the capital's value by 5% each year.

Julie must return to the office after the agreed time.

Capital investment EUR1,000

EUR50 interest for the first Year (EUR1,000 + 5.5%).

EUR52.50 interest in the second year (EUR1.050 + 5.5%).

Mary will receive EUR 1,102.50 in total capital.

We have now realized EUR 2.50 more in this example due to compound interest.

When interest has matured on the underlying capital and is added to it, it is called compound. This creates additional interest in the future.

Are you able to see why compound interest is your best friend?

You are acting as Marie when you deposit money into a bank account. The bank uses the money to perform its credit function, and to lend it to other people and businesses.

You will receive interest on the amount you deposit as a reward.

How to take advantage of compound interest

You must ensure that inflation does not eat into the purchasing power and real value of your money.

You can deposit on one or more accounts to get liquidity. Accounts with limited operations are also available. However, higher interest rates will be recognized.

You could, for example, deposit your emergency fund.

Rest, however, should you invest in a portfolio that provides efficient financial instruments to protect your capital as well as create additional value.

Compounded interest must be used for at least two reasons.

You can save more money while you wait for them to be used.

Protection against inflation.

It is a smart thing to use compound interest to increase your money's value faster and protect it from losing purchasing power.

Keep a small amount of money in bank accounts that offer little or no benefit.

You can save just enough money to cover your daily expenses or for an emergency fund.

Chapter 14: Forex Holding Period

Forex tracing has three options. They are identical to the options in the stock market. These options include intraday trading, longer periods and one-month trading. Let's take a closer look at each.

Intraday trading

Intraday trading is buying and selling currencies at the beginning of the day, and then disposing them at the close of the market. This will ensure that trader does not hold any currency at the close of trading and makes a profit. This method is very popular with traders because it allows them to see an immediate profit and doesn't require any money. This method allows you to trade forex even if your balance is $0. Let's say you buy Yen with dollars. One dollar is equal to fifty yen at the time you bought it. The value of Yen drops to 55 Yen per $1 by the close of the markets. Here, trader can gain 5 Yen more for the same amount he invested, thereby making a profit. The trader can immediately dispose of it and take the profit.

1 month hold

A trader may also use the 1-month hold strategy. This strategy is for traders who are keen to follow a specific pattern. It has been observed that certain currency pairs have a consistent pattern. They will both rise and fall at the exact same time every month. This means that a trader will buy currencies when they are low, and sell them when they rise. This will allow them to keep their profit.

Hold for a long time

If you wish, you can keep the investment longer. You will need to identify the direction of the difference in value. You must get rid of currencies when you reach a goal. The time it takes to get rid of a currency can vary greatly from one currency to the next. It can be held for as little as 6 months or as long for a full year. It all depends on how long the currency is held. Others will not care if they don't reach their profit goal and will simply sell the currency.

These are the time periods you have to choose from in order to hold your currency.

Chapter 15: Turtle Strategy

In the 1980s, Richard Dennis and William Eckhardt shared their stories about their success with the turtle strategy. Dennis believed he could teach anyone how to trade in future markets. Eckhardt countered this belief by stating that Dennis had a special gift that allowed him to be so successful in trading.

Finding the Turtles

To settle the bet, an advertisement was placed in The Wall Street Journal that allowed thousands to apply to Dennis to teach them. Only fourteen people would be selected from the thousands who applied to the "turtle" program. Although it is not known exactly what Dennis used to select his students, it is clear that he asked a series false or true questions.

Trading is a great way to make big money if you can trade at the lows of a downtrend.

It's not useful to monitor every trade in all the markets.

It is a good idea to listen to the opinions of others about the market.

One should risk $2,500 for every trade if one has $10,000 to lose.

When initiating, it is important to know exactly where to liquidate in the event of a loss.

The Turtle method states that 1 and 3 are false, while 2, 4 and 5 are true.

These are the Rules

The turtles of Dennis were shown how to implement a trend-following strategy. To buy future breakouts, they were taught that "trend is your friend". They also learned where to sell short when there was a downside breakout. As an example, suppose you were buying four-week highs at the entry signal.

The trade shown was initiated at a forty-day high. The exit signal is lower than the 20 day low. Dennis kept the exact parameters of the above experiment secret for many years before they were made public. The copyright rules that protect the parameters of the experiment are in "The Complete TurtleTrader" (The Legend, the Lessons and the Results), which Michael Covel published in 2007.

Covel had access to specific rules during the writing of the book.

To make trading decisions, look at the prices and not on television or newspaper commentary.

You should be flexible in setting the parameters of your buy/sell signals. You can test different parameters in different markets to determine which one works best for you.

Plan your exit as you plan your entry. You should know when you will make profits and when to cut losses. (You can learn more about this by reading The Importance of a Profit/Loss Plan (http://www.investopedia.com/articles/01/020701.asp)).

To calculate volatility, use the average true range and adjust your position size accordingly. You should take larger positions in volatile markets to reduce your exposure to volatile markets. You can read more about Measure Volatility with Average True Range. (http://www.investopedia.com/articles/trading/08/average-true-range.asp))

Never risk more than 2% on any single trade.

You must be comfortable with large drawdowns if you want to see big returns.

It worked!

Russell Sands, a former student of Dennis, said that the two turtle classes that he personally trained earned more than $175million in just five years. These results proved that anyone can learn how to trade. Sands agrees that the system works. He says that if you start with $10,000 and follow the turtle rules, your year will end with $25,000

Dennis doesn't have to teach you how to trade turtles. It is a good idea to buy breakouts and close when prices start to consolidate. Because the market is subject to both upwards or downwards trends, any short trades must be done using the same principles. To maximize profits in your trades, your exit signal should be significantly shorter than your initial signal. (Read more about this in The Anatomy of trading Breakouts (http://www.investopedia.com/articles/trading/08/trading-breakouts.asp)).

The turtle experiment was a huge success but there were some drawbacks. Trading systems can experience drawdowns, but trend-following strategies will have more severe problems. This means that most breakouts are false moves and will result in a lot of losing trades. In the end, practitioners should be correct up to half the time to be prepared for large drawdowns.

In order to figure out where you can find more information about the turtle experiment as well as read Dennis story, other success stories from people who learned from Dennis as well as Dennis' rules in order to be a successful trader, you can go to www.turtletrader.com. You will be amazed at the other incredible stories that show how the turtle experiment was used beyond trading.

Chapter 16: Systems And Techniques For Beginners

Trading Systems

A trading system is a set of parameters designed to determine entry and exit for a particular currency or security trade. The parameters used to determine the entry and exit points of trades are recorded in real-time and marked accordingly. This can be used to create a trend on a chart and trigger execution of trades immediately. This saved trader time and eliminated the need to use complicated procedures. Trading systems save traders from using their emotions when trading. They can be outsourced to a brokerage so that they don't have to.

However, each system has its limitations regardless of the type. These systems can be more complicated than others, so traders must understand how they are used to make decisions. To be able to use the system, the trader must also know the technical analysis. Before you adopt a FOREX trading system, make sure to study the technical analysis of the system. You will be able to use the parameters on the charts to help you make trade decisions.

Everyone in the trading industry needs to be able to recognize when it is time to make a move. The system that you use should not hinder your ability to do this. Most traders use a customized system to ensure they understand the system. A system that is used for day trading may not work for swing trading. For traders who trade using fundamental strategies, a system that relies on patterns for trading may not be the best. You should therefore know your best strategies and your trading skills before you choose a system. Many systems are limited in their ability to work for a certain period of time because the FOREX market changes constantly. Your system should be capable of adapting to the changes by constant updates.

Otherwise, it will become obsolete and can't be used in new trading markets.

Many traders have developed systems that are specialized in specific trading strategies. If you trade events that impact FOREX trading, the Geopolitical Turbulence trading system can be used in your trades. For example, speeches by presidents and governors or conferences organized by the central banks of countries whose currencies are in the FOREX exchange market will all have a microeconomic impact on FX markets. These macroeconomic indicators can strike at the most unexpected times and are unpredictable. Geopolitical conflict is another example of unexpected changes in the market that surprise traders. If you decide to use the geopolitical trade system, ensure that you have the ability to monitor and follow the developments in the country of origin for the currencies you wish to pair. This will help you to make decisions that are both certain and beneficial. You should not wait for an event before you make a decision about buying one or both of the currencies you wish to pair. Instead, buy one currency of each pair anc be ready to take action in the event of a destabilizing event.

Candlestick patterns and moving averages are another trading method. There are many types of moving averages. The most common is the simple one, which is a study for a set period. The best way to use this system is to first find the right moving average for you and then search for candlestick pattern that match the moving average. It is important to be able to recognize the possible candlestick patterns around a moving average, and when they are most effective to use. A candlestick must also meet these criteria to be more successful. If you are a beginner and you want to learn how to use the simple moving average and a candlestick, you should first practice the move on a demo account. Once you have perfected the skill, you can then transfer it into a real investment account.

Some traders choose scalping to be their trading strategy. They can trade this system. This system requires you to generate trading signals using mainly the fundamental analysis. Automated systems can do the analysis and give you signals when to buy or sell. As long as you learn how to trade manually, automated trading is best for beginners. The automated system does not allow you to gain the skills. It is possible to learn trading the hard way, but it can be frustrating. This skill will allow you to analyze and determine trade signals. However, the FOREX market can be volatile and your system could become outdated if it is not constantly updated. There are many systems that allow scalping with a specific currency pair. The most popular is the USD/JPY EMA scalping system. These currency pairs are moderately volatile, and have moderate risk. If you do your research, everyone can create a trading system that works. You can choose any pair you like, except the USD/JPY option. As long as your chosen pair has characteristics that allow you to manage trades and minimize losses, you are good to go.

These trading systems aren't the only ones we have. There are many others. And, as mentioned earlier, all depend on the trader. It is important to understand how the currency trade parameters work and when exit points are available. Start by learning how to trade, and then use your knowledge to choose the right trading strategy. You may need to pay attention to certain trading systems. This should be taken into consideration when choosing the right system.

Trading Techniques for Beginners

FOREX is the largest financial market in the world. There are many trading methods available. This includes selling and buying securities, including stocks, softs and metals. Different platforms and systems are used to ensure that trading activities can be executed efficiently. Different strategies use different strategies. They speculate on the best way to maximize profits and make predictions. Day trading, swing trading and position trading are the four main techniques.

Day Trading Techniques

Day trading involves opening trading positions, then closing them all. Trades can be closed at the end of the trading day. This type of trading requires the trader to have extensive FOREX trading experience. Day traders must consider different strategies before making a decision. These strategies will help them to choose the most successful strategies. Technical indicators are sometimes used by traders to calculate the best time frames for entry and exit. Others rely on their intuitions to determine the best move that will bring in profits. This technique allows traders to use price action characteristics to hold positions and trade currencies. They rarely use fundamental information. Day traders make their profits by focusing on volatility and the day range. Trades are established by the trader moving quickly in and out of the trade. This technique of trading is important because it considers the liquidity and volume of currency being traded. This allows traders to focus on currencies that have a high volume and a wide range of prices. Day traders are attracted to events that have a short-term effect on currency prices and volumes. Day traders find it beneficial to trade news about certain economic aspects, such as interest rates and the release of data on corporate earnings.

Use the Position Trading Method

ForeX position trading involves taking or holding a trade position for a longer period. This can last for years, months or even weeks. This technique does not take into account the currency price fluctuations in the short term or the daily news releases. This technique doesn't make traders active as they can only make a few positions over the course of a year. To determine the security movements towards a particular trend, they use monthly or weekly price action charts analysis. They also use primary trends to maximize their profits. Position technique is different from day trading. It uses both technical and fundamental indicators analysis. This gives traders a clear view of the FOREX market, which allows them to make informed decisions.

Swing trading techniques can be used

This is a trading strategy that traders use to make profits by taking overnight positions that last for a few weeks. This strategy mainly uses fundamental indicators analysis. It includes analysis of patterns and trends in currency prices. Technical analysis is also used to determine the short term momentum price. They look for currencies that can make a dramatic move in a very short time. They like trading currencies that have large price swings in a short time span. This makes them spend many weeks, if not months, monitoring the market to determine the price change. These traders sell their currencies when the price swings upwards. If the swing stops, they stop selling or the trade is over. They are able to focus on the given assets to better understand the movement. This is in contrast to investors who buy and hold. This trading technique is a good option for traders looking to make a living. They have lower risks than other trading methods. The trader doesn't need to constantly monitor real-time data to analyze it and determine when to make a profit. This technique is suitable for people who trade part-time.

Scalp Trading

This type of trading involves trading currencies. The trader holds the position for a brief time in the hope that he/she will be able to move on to a profitable trading position. With the hopes of making a substantial amount from small percentages of the market profits, traders may take multiple positions within a single day. The trader uses functional strategies to maximize the opportunities that are available in the market. Hotkeys can be used to execute desired trades at the computer. The automated trading system, on the other hand uses established rules and guidelines to determine a trade signals.

FOREX trading is an extremely profitable market, but there are also many risks. It is crucial for traders to evaluate their trading skills and decide if they want to trade swing, day, scalping, or position.

Chapter 17: Building A Strategy

First, it is important to determine if you are a professional trader and if you are a novice. Second, there is no way for a trader, regardless of how smart or lucky they may be, to succeed without a strategy.

Jose Raul Capablanca: "To improve your game, study the endgame first. For whereas the endings are easily studied and mastered, the middle and opening must be studied in relation the the endgame.'

Without a firm and well-thought out strategy, no trader can be successful.

Particularly if you deal in foreign exchange markets. Profits can be as high as 80%.

Success is directly related to the strategy chosen - this is the development path that is selected. This success is determined by the selection of resources, coordination and the planning of corresponding actions.

All spheres of human existence, including financial, have been impacted by the term strategy. It is defined as captainship if we look at it from the military sphere. The strategy of winning war is military strategy. The military commander chose it based on his knowledge, skills, traditions, as well as his past successes and failures.

It is therefore impossible to find the strategy science that you need, if you only have access to literature sources. Strategy is not a set of algorithms or models. The instrument is knowledge, and the strategist is a creator.

Strategy is a plan that aims to achieve a goal. It is derived from the Greek strategia (strategia), which means "office of general command, generalship, and general general".

The solution to intermediate tactical schemes is what makes strategy work.

Target is the key. "What's the best way to achieve your goals without spending a lot of time and resources?"

This question is answered by Strategy

The most important thing in selecting a Forex trading strategy for you is to determine your goals. The best traders have a strategy. They take a strategy that they like, modify it, and add personalities to it until it is no longer similar to the original. They keep trying new things, and learning from each other to create their trading strategies.

The goal is to have a risk level that is proportional to investment returns. This is the most important rule in foreign exchange markets. The higher the risk, the greater the profit. It is important that trader determine his risk level. You can choose to trade with high-risk trading that could result in huge profits or trading with lower risk but steady profit. This will determine the style of your future strategy. Traders-conservators, on the other hand, will opt for the conservative strategy. Risky traders will continue to follow the aggressive strategy.

defensive, long-term position.

It is possible to make profits on the forex market. There is a high risk involved in internet trading as with any other form of trading. This is something that every trader must remember. Any trading strategy should include money management and risk management.

Tacitus: "Even the bravest of men are scared by sudden terrors."

Trading involves losses. It is

It is important to not only think about it, but also to be aware of it.

You are able to

You can overcome the crisis by patience.

Do not panic, but you can be calm.

Know-nothing

Person. A correctly selected strategy will work.

This will help to reduce the potential losses.

This will al'ow you to minimize your losses as well as provide additional information.

Losses can help you improve your strategies

An investor who is a good one realizes that there are always losses.

This is only a part of the game.

Defining, challenging and accepting.

Profits can be made by learning from past losses.

Trading is a new industry. New traders should establish their goals, position and follow them throughout their trading activity. There are many strategies and methods for currency trading. They correspond to the number of traders.

Practically every trader believes that his strategy is the best and most effective.

And the best.Forex Trading for The Advance Binary Option Trader

"In the moment to act, remember the value silence and order."

Phormio at Athens

One or more cannot be named.

Strategies that will work

Unchangeable and that will continue

You will be a constant success.

Any strategy can bring success.

If you put it to the test, you will reap the rewards

It can be adjusted to the market

Conditions Markets

Always changing and always evolving.

A good strategist is a con

Continuously updating and

Adjusting his strategy to the market. A long-term trader will eventually have many variations of his strategy so that he can adapt to changing markets.

Chapter 18: What Is Forex Trading?

First, let me say that I am grateful for the opportunity to read your book. We will be discussing the basics of forex trading in this chapter.

What is Forex trading?

Forex (Foreign Exchange Market), is the largest financial market in the world. Forex trading is Currency exchange trading. It is vital for currencies to exist on this planet. People will not be able buy or sell goods if they don't exist. These goods cannot be sold or bought in the country where they are manufactured. They must also be purchased from another country. Let's say you have a line in Germany, and want to purchase a laptop from China. German currency is Euro and Chinese currency Yuan. The Chinese seller won't accept Euros as payment if you want to purchase a laptop. Instead, he would prefer Dollars. Dollars are the most commonly accepted currency. He will also want Yuan in his

Chinese bank account. To pay the Chinese seller, you will need to convert your Euro into Dollars. This is where you need to be aware that your currency will be converted to a certain exchange rate at the moment of conversion. This "rate" will always result in a difference between the currencies' values. This will always be an advantage to one country, and a disadvantage for another. We could continue to analyze the situation.

One Euro is worth 20 Yuan. The German trader can exchange 1 euro for 20 Yuan or 100 euros for 2000 Yuan. The Yuan is more popular than the Euro in this instance, meaning that Germany is better at forex trading. However, a Chinese trader would need to spend a lot more to purchase wine from Germany if the rates were different. This is only an example. Rates can vary greatly. It could be either higher or lower in value.

Here, the buyer wants to exchange their money to purchase something from a foreign seller. However, Forex is not always traded just for this purpose. You can also trade it to profit from the differences in value. If you play the game correctly, you could make huge profits. However, there are some things you need to know before you can invest in Forex markets.

We will show you how to do this throughout the book. We will now look at the basics of forex trading in this next segment.

Forex trading concepts

Majors

The majors are the first concept you need to understand. The Forex market regularly trades the major currencies as the majors. There are thousands of shares available on the stock market that a trader can choose to invest in. This can confuse traders and lead to them making the wrong investments. This problem can be solved in Forex markets, since there are some major currencies you can trade in regularly. These are based upon trends.

Once you have figured out which countries offer the greatest over- and undervalued benefits, these can be used to help you make informed decisions. Below is a list of 8 countries you can look to for the best profit.

The United States of America

Canada

Europe

United Kingdom

Switzerland

Australia

New Zealand

Japan

These 8 countries are known as the big 8, because they have the most advanced financial markets and/or manufacturing capacities. Their currencies are always in demand and can be exchanged. Your investment will be protected if you exchange these currencies at the right time. You must monitor the economic situation of each country to ensure that you are always in the know.

Sell and buy

It is important to realize that Forex markets work in simultaneous buying and selling. You will need to sell your currency if you wish to purchase another currency. If you have physical Euros, this is simple to understand. You can walk into a Bank to exchange physical dollars for your Euros. You can sell your Euros or buy Dollars. You can buy and sell in one transaction.

Forex traders trade Forex symbols known as "pairs". This means that when you buy one currency, you automatically sell it. The simple example above shows that you traded EUR/USD. This symbol is used in a trading platform to purchase Euros (in USD) or Dollars ($ in Euros). The same principle applies to all symbols and pairs. If you "buy" the symbol, you're buying the first currency. If you "sell" the symbol, you're buying the second currency. This concept is essential to trading Forex.

Based on the difference between the currencies, you will need to calculate the basis points. This can be done by looking at the trends in the rates of the currencies. Basis points are a measure of interest or percentages you will need to calculate before making a deal. This will allow you to calculate your profit.

Rate of Return

Forex market returns are very high. This means you can make a large profit or lose a lot of money depending on how much you invest. People have made millions just by investing a few hundred dollars or a thousand dollars. If you invest in the market correctly, this is possible. Let's suppose you invest $10 and get a $1000 return. This is possible in the currency markets. But if you do it wrong, you could lose a lot of your money. You need to keep track of changes in currency values as they are volatile. You should look for currencies that are temporarily undervalued. That way you can expect a large change in currency value to close the transaction at your desired profit. You can sell the currencies if you feel they are going to cost you money.

Dual benefits

When you invest in the forex market, you get dual benefits. This is also known as the Currency Carry Trade. Two benefits can be derived from the Currency Carry Trade. Let's take an example. Let's suppose a Chinese trader converts 5000 Yuan to dollars and purchases a bond with the dollar's worth. If the exchange rate between the two countries is the same, the trader will earn 5% interest on the bond. The trader will earn a 50% profit if the exchange rate between the two countries remains the same. The trader can also make a profit by selling the bond later. This is where it becomes important to remember that the exchange rate between them should not change. Otherwise, the trader could lose money. Currency rates that are highly volatile pose a high risk. It is impossible to predict how rates will change and you could lose a lot of money if you do. The rate difference usually takes place over many years, and not in a very short time.

OTC

Forex trades OTC (over-the-counter) and is not traded on the Stock Market, which deals with Financial Instruments that are regulated. The currency is not considered "financial instrument" in many countries, and therefore are not regulated. An Electronic Communication Network (ECN) allows banks and brokers to trade currencies. This is a different medium than a stock exchange such as NYSE or AMEX. The trade will be handled by a dealer, with no central control. This is exactly the way penny stocks and bonds are traded. It is important to research how to trade in your local market. The process varies from one country to the next. Look for dealers who can help you obtain these currencies. This network connects all banks and brokers that are authorized to trade currencies. To be able to place orders over the internet, you will need to have an authorized broker or bank.

These are the basic concepts of forex you need to know if you want to trade it. These concepts will serve as your guide for forex trad ng.

Chapter 19: What Is Forex Trade?

Forex is a term that means foreign currency and can be used to refer, in exchange, the purchase or sale one currency. Because it includes people, companies, as well as countries, it is the most traded market in the world. Participating in the global forex market is when you travel on a tour or convert your US dollars to euros.

Millions of trades are made every day on the Forex currency exchange market. The phrase "Forex" starts with two phrases: "Foreign "and" exchange. Forex is not like other trading systems such as the stock market. It does not involve formal or physical trading in goods. Forex is a currency trading system that works in different currencies. It involves buying, selling, and trading with other economies all over the world. Forex trading is a global trading market. It operates 24 hours a days, five days per week. Forex is also free from any control agency, making it the only true free-market financial trading platform. It is difficult to manipulate or control the monetary markets by manipulating exchange rates. The Forex market is the largest market in the world, thanks to all its benefits and wide participation spectrum. Each day, the Forex market is home to trades worth between 1 trillion and 1,5 trillion dollars.

Forex is based on the idea of "free-floating currencies". This can be best described as currencies that are not supported by specific products like gold or silver. A company like Forex wouldn't have existed before 1971 without the global "Bretton Woods" agreement. This agreement indicated that all countries would try to keep their currency values close to the US dollar. The gold value was reserved for each country. The 1971 Bretton Woods Agreement has been cancelled. The United States ran a huge deficit during the Vietnam war and began printing more paper currency than gold, which led to an incredibly high rate of inflation. The Bretton Woods Agreement was abandoned by all major currencies in 1976. They switched to a free-floating currency system. The free-floating system meant that each country's currency could have distinct fluctuations depending on the state of its economy.

Forex is a significant part of some of the wealthiest people in the world. Warren Buffett, the richest man on the planet, has made more than $20 trillion in Forex trading in different currencies. His revenues include well over 100 million USD per quartile of Forex trading profits.

George Soros, another prominent name in currency trading, is estimated to have made more than $1 Billion in profit in a single trading day in 1992. These types of trades are rare but he still managed to make $7 trillion in three decades of Forex trading. George Soros' liberal strategy to Forex trading shows that it doesn't need to be risky to make money. He removes large amounts of the industry's income, but the pattern of its assets seems to still point upwards.

Keep your emotions out of Forex Trading

The biggest problem you will face when you first start trading Forex is not finding the best Forex broker or the most profitable Forex trading strategy. The Forex markets are not conspiring against you and you don't need any hidden knowledge to succeed. Although it may sound cliché, your emotions are the greatest obstacle to Forex profits.

What systems can and cannot do for you

Don't get me confused. To trade Forex effectively, you will need a reliable Forex broker and a profitable Forex trading platform. There are many great Forex brokers and profitable Forex trading systems, but few Forex traders make it big. Why is this? They trade without feeling.

Emotional self-control is key to successful Forex trading. As well as proper decision making, these are two essential components. Trading a handbook plan like a pro is possible if you are able to manage your emotions quickly. If you are unable to regulate your emotions during or after a trade then it is important that you be open with yourself. You should not trade instant Forex trading strategies until you are ready.

Automated Forex trading systems can help you distinguish emotions from trading. Once you have learned how to manage them properly, your system will take all your decisions.

After you have a proven trading strategy in place, you can start Forex trading. However, you should not be putting all your resources into your trading plan. People who start trading Forex can fall into the trap of becoming greedy and risking all their hard-earned money. They are likely to make beginner mistakes because they are inexperienced with Forex trading.

Instead of focusing on making a lot of money with Forex, you should learn how to trade Forex. After you have accumulated enough Forex trading knowledge over a period of at least a few month, that's what you should expect. When you first start trading Forex, you want to only invest what you can afford to trade. Why? Why?

Forex traders who are just starting out need to learn how to manage their emotions. It's not uncommon to start a Forex trading business while still studying. Many traders are skilled in trading both manual and automated strategies to maximize their profits while minimizing the risks.

My advice to Forex traders is to be open about your plans and aspirations. You don't need to be ready to trade manual Forex. It doesn't matter if you use a profitable Forex trading program. You may also find that you are able to build Forex portfolios to maximize your returns and eliminate your business emotions.

Thad B. is a certified trading scheme developer and has managed numerous lucrative trading systems for private investors over the years. He is an expert in Forex trading systems and has many helpful resources available to any serious Forex system trader.

You don't need to invest millions to make Forex a profitable business.

Many people have reported that they received grants ranging from $10,000 to $100 with funds from any country. Forex is a popular location for traders of all economic levels, from the less well-off to those at the top of the income ladder to the most wealthy. For those on the lower end of the scale, access to the Forex market represents a recent growth. Different businesses have developed a more compassionate approach to business over the past decades. This has allowed for lower initial yields and greater effectiveness in the current industry. You can now get started regardless of your financial situation.

Although you can immediately start trading Forex, it is best to get a better understanding of the intricacies before you begin.

Forex work can be lucrative and enjoyable. However, it is important to understand how the Forex scheme works in order to find a job. As with all lucrative professions, you will need to practice a lot to become a Forex professional. Many blogs offer mock exercises in Foreign Exchange.

A story about two Forex traders just starting out

Let me tell you a story about Jim and Tom, two Forex traders. They have just finished reading a lot about Forex. Both spent hours on the internet trying to learn about currency trading and how they could make some quick profits. You can easily increase your income with all the marketing messages they send. Although there is some risk involved, the benefits are too great to ignore. They decide to both try Forex and see what happens.

Both children are extremely motivated and want to make Forex as successful as possible. Each of them will invest $1000 of their money in currency trading. If they lose $1000, they'll quit Forex and reevaluate whether or not to try again. They both invested a thousand dollars to demonstrate their commitment to making Forex work for them.

To start: Tom will take all of his $1000 and transfer it to an online retail Forex broker. Tom will make all the commercial decisions. To see if he can get any valuable advice, he will do his research and sleep on Forex forums and blogs.

Jim is determined to find a clear path. He's as determined as Tom and is aware of the complex Forex market. However, he also understands the limitations of his knowledge. He takes $900 and transfers it to the same Tom Forex broker wholesale. In order to gain access to tools and assets, he spends $100 more to build a company. He used to trade stocks daily and knows from personal experience the benefits these funds and tools can bring (especially if one knows the strings).

Month 1: Tom jumps into currency trading immediately. He started his first trade in the negative but quickly moved to the west. Before he could publish his selling request, he had already spent $100. Although he had some small profitable trades, his trading history was very similar to his first trading. Although many trades began well, he would eventually lose money. He didn't have enough knowledge to fully understand the reasons. Tom's first month of currency trading saw his trading register drop to $400.

Jim went through some studies, and found Forex with Ambush. This page was affiliated with Ambush and sends its workers hints. He was struck by the fact that their trade messages were accurate to 99.9%. How could they make such a bold declaration? Jim did a little more digging and received a lot of positive feedback from his current staff. Jim was also influenced by Forex Ambush. They are offered a 7-day trial at a fraction of the normal price.

Jim had seven days to test Forex Ambush, which cost less than $20 and provided 99.9% accurate trade messages. He is enthusiastic about it. He had $900 in his Forex trading account, but he still had $80+ available in case Forex Ambush didn't help.

Forex Ambush sent Jim an email with a trading message on the next day. Although he was new to Forex, he received an email from Forex Ambush with a trading message. He kept the bold precision declaration in mind and placed it in his possession. Jim had already made $145 profit the day before his business was closed. He was thrilled! Jim signed up to continue his participation in Forex Ambush after the 7-day court ended. While not all trading messages yielded profits every time, most of them did. He's also had very few casualties. Jim had $1750 left in his Forex trading account after a month.

Month 2: Tom felt deflated. In a matter of a month, his net worth had increased from $1000 to $400. To try and return his money, he made higher-valued, more risky trades. He was left with $0 at the end of the month. Tom was angry and annoyed. He quit Forex again, claiming it was a fraud to anyone who would listen and save their money.

Jim was ninety-nine in the cloud. He received $1750 instead of the $900 he originally received. Not only did he still receive emails with trade clues via Forex Ambush but he also looked at several other Forex trading platforms. After a month of profitable trades, he had a better understanding of the Forex market and was more confident. Jim's initial trading proposal was $2355 at month 2.

The most striking thing about Jim's story was his ability to do all of this in his spare time. He still worked full-time to pay for his travel expenses. He considered everything he did in Forex to be extra. He considered trading Forex as a way to quit his job. He is happy with his current job and the security it provides.

Moral of the story? If you are looking to excel in any area you don't have much knowledge or experience in, it is strongly recommended that you invest in the tools and money to increase your chances of success.

Tell yourself, "Would you like to be Tom? Needy, upset and swearing that Forex is a scam?" Would you rather spend your money on tools that will allow you to perform better and make more income? You can make Forex money if you are serious about it. Then you need to find the best Forex trading system.

Investors benefit from a healthy dose of trepidation. Complex investment products and active trading strategies don't belong in most portfolios.

Maybe you already have a balanced portfolio and are looking for an adventure with extra cash. Forex trading is lucrative if you are able to understand what you are doing. It requires only a small initial investment.

There are many ways that Forex trading is different from stock trading:

Forex trades can be made over-the-counter -- trader to trader, through forex brokers or dealers -- and not through a central exchange.

Forex traders can trade across time zones. The forex market is available 24 hours a days, five days per week.

Currencies can only be traded in pairs and prices are quoted in pairs.

The currency prices change rapidly, but only in small increments. This makes it difficult for investors to make a profit on small trades. This is why currency trades almost always involve leverage or borrowing money from the broker.

Forex can be traded in pairs so you will always exchange the same currency from one currency to another. The "majors", 7 currencies: the Euro (EUR), United States

(USD), Canadian, British (GBP), Australian, AUD, Japanese Yen(JPY), Swiss (CHF), and Canadian (CAD), which are most traded. These currencies together with the US dollars make up the "major pairs."

What is the Forex Market?

Currencies can be traded on the foreign currency market. The vast majority of people in the world have significant foreign currency currencies. Foreign exchange and trade must both be exchanged. If you reside in the U.S., the company you purchase cheese from from or you must pay the French for it in Euros (EUR). The US importer must exchange euros for equivalent US dollars (USD). This is also true for the trip. A French tourist cannot pay for the pyramids of Egypt in euros because this currency is not accepted locally. The tourist will need to exchange EUR for local currency at the current exchange rates, which in this instance is the Egyptian pound.

One of the most important aspects of the world market is that there is no central market for currency trading. Instead, electronic currency trading (OTCs), takes place via computer networks among traders around the globe and is not done on central exchanges. The market is open 24/7, 5 and 1/2 days per week and currencies are traded around the globe in major financial centers like London, New York, Tokyo and Zurich. The forex market opens in Tokyo and Hong Kong at the end of the US trade day. This means that the forex market can be extremely active with constantly changing prices.

Most providers divide pairs into one of the following categories to keep things organized:

Major pairs - Seven currencies make up 80% of forex trading worldwide. Include EUR/USD, USD/JPY and GBP/USD.

These minor pairs are less traded and often feature major currencies against one another instead of the US Dollar. This includes: EUR/GBP and EUR/CHF.

Exotics - A major currency that is not a currency from a small emerging or developing economy. Included: USD/PLN; GBP/MXN; EUR/CZK

Pairs classified by region, such as Australasia or Scandinavia, are called regional pairs. Included: EUR/NOK; AUD/NZD; AUD/SGD

Banks and individuals often transact forex by buying foreign currencies that are higher than the currency they sell. If you have ever exchanged one currency for another, such as when you travel, then you are likely to have done a forex transaction.

Understanding forex lot sizes

The "lot trades forex" refers to micro lots of 1,000 currency units. A mini lot is 10,000 units and a standard lot at 100,000 units. A larger lot size means that you are taking on more risk. Individual investors should not trade standard lots.

As a beginner, we recommend that you keep on the micro lot.

It's a great place to observe that most forex brokers offer demo trading accounts to investors.

Play money is more entertaining than real money, especially when you're just starting out.

A series of tips has been created to help you navigate the whole process. While you may already be familiar with how currency exchange rates fluctuate, the benefits of being a Forex tracer are different than what you might think. Chapter 20: Basic Day Trading Strategies & Terms

How to determine the price target

These are the most popular strategies for choosing your price target.

1. Scalping refers to the act of selling a property as soon it becomes profitable. When profitability is established, the price target should be set immediately.

Scalper is a day trader who buys and sells stock consistently, often hundreds of times per day. Scalpers make small profits from each trade which leads to a big profit at the close of business. Being a scalper has its disadvantages. The scalper is always looking at the monitor and trying to find small changes. For their many transactions, the scalper could be charged hundreds of dollars. Scalpers may sign up for investment accounts where their fees are determined by the volume of trades. This ensures that their monthly profits don't exceed the brokerage fees.

Level II quotes must be available to scalers during trades and asks. They also need charts such as the candlestick charts and reliable phone systems. Spreads used to be offered in decimal points, but now they are offered in whole cents. Scalping is more expensive and has lower margins.

2. Fading refers to a trade in which stocks are sold short before the price is ready. This strategy is most effective when it is not too late.

Stocks have been overbought

The early buyers are anxious and ready to sell

The existing holders are now scared

As buyers move again, the price target is set.

3. Daily Pivots allow you to buy at the Low of Day and sell at the High of Day. Because the stock is volatile, the pivot point will be the price target. The stock will fluctuate and move between the low and high of the day. This is an example for stock volatility.

These are the standard calculations for Pivot points

A pivot point refers to the point at which a security's price moves. These prices are used to calculate the pivot area from the closing, high, and low stock prices. These prices can be accessed from either the hourly or daily charts. The daily charts are used by most traders. These findings can then be applied to intraday charts every hour or more often. A full day of pivot points will be more accurate than a sample from a quarter-hour chart. The more data collected, the better the results.

Formulas to establish pivot points

Central Pivot Point, (P) = (High + Lower + Close) / 3.

The following formulae are used to calculate support and resistance levels from this pivot point:

Support and resistance at the first level:

First Resistance (R1) = (2*P). - Low

Second Support (S1) = (2*P). - High

The second level of support or resistance is also calculated in the following:

Second Resistance (R2) = (R1–S1)

Second Support (S2) = p - (R1 - S1)

4. Momentum refers to trading on strong trends with high volumes. You might buy the news release, then sell when the trend reaches its peak and reverses. You may

also lose your position at the peak of the price point. When volume drops and the bearish trend starts, that is when the price target becomes a reality.

The day begins with the analysis of the stocks that the momentum trader has selected to focus on. This is done by looking at the momentum indicator. The momentum indicator measures the cumulative net change in the stock's closing and opening prices over a predetermined period. The price chart shows the momentum line. It has a zero axis and positive values for upward or bullish movements. Negative values are for bearish movements.

Momentum trader is searching for breakout stocks on Level II screen where there is evidence of a push. He expects the breakout to be in line with the trend, so that he can ride the upward or down momentum. He sells his stock at the saturation point when he believes that the stock will turn the trend around.

Day trading strategists choose the entry points as volume increases, and the exits when there are differences.

Traditional trading methods include:

1. Fundamental Trading

Fundamentalists, including Warren Buffet, the most well-known and successful trader, trade companies using fundamental analysis. They examine corporate financial reports to determine actual or expected earnings, stock splits and reorganizations, and then trade them.

Fundamental analysis involves using financial reports and business data to determine a security's worth. Fundamental analysis is used by most financial analysts to evaluate stocks. However, it can also be used for other types of security.

A fundamental analysis of ABC bonds' value can be done by an investor. This involves looking at economic factors such as interest rates and the overall economy. It also considers the credit rating changes that may occur. This method is used to assess DEF stocks by using revenue, earnings and future growth. It also returns on equity. Profit margins are used to calculate the potential for future expansion. Fundamental analysis is focused on the financial statements of a company that issues the stock being evaluated.

Swing Trading

Fundamental traders are called swing traders, and they hold positions for longer than one day. Sometimes even four to five days. Swing traders are the majority of fundamentalists. Because changes in corporate fundamentals can take several days, or even weeks, to create a price movement that is sufficient to allow trader to make a reasonable profit, swing traders are most often swing traders. Swing traders use technical analysis to find stocks that have short-term price momentum. These traders look at stock performance patterns and price trends.

Stop Losses

Margin traders are more susceptible to price fluctuations than cash traders. It is important to place an automatic stop loss execution order.

You can set two stop losses:

1. Set an automatic stop loss at a price that is within your risk tolerance. This should be located at the price level where you have established a limit for your maximum loss.

2. 2.Set a mental stop-loss if the trade is not in line with your entry criteria. If it goes south, you should immediately exit the trade. Don't wait for the trade to turn.

No matter what, set a daily maximum loss. Once you reach this limit, quit your job immediately. You can take the day off and go to your spouse, children, or friend. This will allow you to put aside trading. Don't try to make up for your losses by trading one more time. It will cause you to lose your strategy and make it difficult for yourself to recoup your losses. You will have a miserable day, lose your job and may even feel bad when you get home from work. It would be much more enjoyable to spend quality time with loved ones.

Slippage

Slippage refers to the unfortunate occurrence that occurs to all traders, regardless of type. It is when you receive a lower price than you expected on your trade entry or exit. Slippage can happen in any type of trade, whether it's futures, options, forex, or stocks. Here's why:

Your expected cost would be $49.37 if the bid-ask spread is between $49.36 and $49.37 for your stock. If you buy 500 shares, that is $49.37. Your trade could be $0.63 more expensive if the market price changes to $50.00 within a fraction of a second after your transmission. This is called slippage.

Slippage and Order Types

Market orders are used by traders to prevent slippage. Market orders can be used to both enter and exit a position. Slippage can occur at either end of the trade.

Limit orders are a strategy that prevents slippage. Limit orders are only filled at the price that you have specified or at a higher price. This will prevent slippage and also eliminate the possibility of a trade if you don't get the price that you want.

Entry of Positions with a Limit Order

A limit order may prevent you from missing potential trade opportunities. However, it can also reduce your vulnerability to unanticipated loss by avoiding "overpaying" for the trade. You can control your trade by using a limit order to enter a trade.

Exiting positions with a Limit Order

Place a limit order at the "target price" when a trade is moving in your favor. We bought shares at $50.00 on our previous order. Let's place our limit orders to sell our shares for $50.15. Limit orders will not be sold until they find a buyer for $50.15. This is your exit position.

Big Window for Slippage

Slippage is most likely to occur around major new events. Avoid trading during the FOMC minutes and earnings announcements of your stock company. Slippage is a common occurrence during these announcements.

Day Trading Entry Strategies

Two factors are important for day traders to be successful in trading:

liquidity

Volatility

Liquidity

Liquidity allows you to trade at a fair price.

Volatility

Volatility allows you to choose a price range in which to buy the stock. Profit opportunities are greater if there is more volatility.

Identifying the Best Entry Points to Trades

Once you have found a product that meets your criteria, you can identify your entry points. These are three tools that you can use to identify your entry points.

Candles provide analysis of price action (also known as Intraday Candlestick charts).

ECN and Level II show instant orders in real-time

The News Service provides live news updates as they happen.

These are the factors to consider when analyzing intraday candlestick charts

Look for dojis and engulfings on the Candlestick Patterns page.

Look for triangles and trend lines in the Technical Analysis

Look for decreasing and increasing volumes in the Volume section.

Candlestick offers many options for finding an entry point.

The candlestick chart shows the trader the following information: the opening price of stock, closing price of stock, intraday high or low price. These lines, also known as shadows, represent the high- and low stock share prices for the day. The stock's opening and closing prices are indicated by the thicker bars (called real body). The shares closed the day at the High Of the Day and Low of the Day, respectively, if there is a thin line between the bars. A cross/plus sign is used to indicate days when the stock closed and opened at the same price. The green lines indicate days when the stock closed above its opening price. The red bars represent days when the stock closed below its opening price. This means that it is losing value.

This candlestick chart is known as a "hanging guy". The price moved higher than the close price and then fell for the remainder of the day. This is volatility. The hanging man indicates a downward trend. This is the second blue box. It shows a candlestick chart known as a hammer. This is a reverse of a bullish trend.

In this example, we will use the doji reverse pattern strategy.

The components of the doji reverse pattern

You should look for patterns that include the following components:

You should look for a volume spike. This indicates that traders are buying to support the price. This can be found on the doji candle, or any of the following.

For price support, we look at the previous low or high of each day. (LOD, HOD)

We will be examining the Level II marker. This indicates the open orders as well as the order size.

These steps will determine if the Doji is in a turnaround. If so, it will be possible to trade.

The Elliott Wave Pattern: Components

Based on crowd psychology, the Elliott wave pattern was created in 1930s. It moves between optimism and pessimism through waves in a sequence. Elliot believes that market prices alternate between the corrective and impulsive phases. Five lower degree waves characterize impulses. Waves 1, 3, 5, and 5 are impulse waves, while waves 2 and 4 represent correcting waves. This is the pattern in a bull market. However, the trend is down in a bear market. The trend is always followed by the corrective waves that oppose it.

Wave 1 marks the beginning of a bullish market, but it is rarely visible. Wave 2 is the continuation of the bull market but traders are more bearish. Wave 3 changes the tide, and the market moves bullish. Wave 4 is corrective, and can move in any direction. Wave 5 is bullish and leads this trend.

The corrective waves.

Wave A is bearish.

Wave B is bullish.

Wave C is very bearish, and everyone is firmly entrenched.

The Seven-Day Extension Fade on the Candlestick chart

This strategy is simple as it only measures candlesticks and price. There are no contingent factors.

Strategy Rules

This strategy's accuracy is further cemented by the seventh candle coinciding with a key technical level.

Guidelines for Long Trades

1. Seven consecutive bars of weakness are required. Each bar will close below its predecessor close.

2. 2.

3. Stop at the lowest bar, minus $0.01.

4. Your first target is the amount you are willing to risk. To break even, move the stop at the other half.

5. The second target is three times the amount of capital at risk. (3%) of capital

Short Trade Rules

1. Find seven bars of strength in succession, where each bar closes higher than the previous close.

2. 2.

3. Your stop should be at the seventh bar's highest point plus 10 pips.

4. Your first target should be your maximum risk, not exceeding $300 or 1% capital. To break even, move the stop on half of the remaining target.

5. 5. The second target is three-times the amount at risk, which equals $900 and 3% capital.

Conclusion

You can see that we covered many topics in this book. We talked about Forex Trading and how to start Forex Trading. We also provided information you won't find anywhere else online.

We have already said that finding information online about Forex Trading is not a good idea. The information available online is outdated. This book provided all the information you needed to succeed in Forex Trading. That is because the information online is not up-to-date.

You should use this information to your advantage. If you don't understand something in the book, you can always refer back to it. You will have a better chance of success in Forex Trading if you understand the information in this book. You don't have to make money.